HAUNTED ROANOKE

L.B. Taylor Jr.

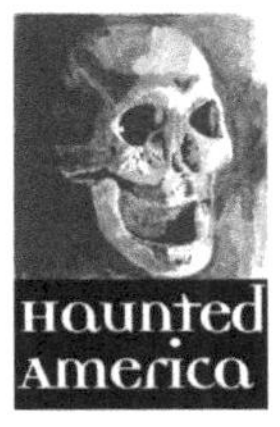

Published by Haunted America
A Division of The History Press
Charleston, SC 29403
www.historypress.net

First published 2013

Manufactured in the United States

ISBN 978.1.60949.943.3

Library of Congress Cataloging-in-Publication Data

Taylor, L. B.
Haunted Roanoke / L.B. Taylor Jr.
pages cm
Includes bibliographical references.
ISBN 978-1-60949-943-3
1. Ghosts--Virginia--Roanoke. 2. Haunted places--Virginia--Roanoke. 3. Parapsychology--Virginia--Roanoke. 4. Roanoke (Va.)--Social life and customs. 5. Roanoke (Va.)--Biography. I. Title.
BF1472.U6T3954 2013
133.109755'791--dc23
2013018287

Notice: The information in this book is true and complete to the best of our knowledge. It is offered without guarantee on the part of the author or The History Press. The author and The History Press disclaim all liability in connection with the use of this book.

CONTENTS

Contents

INTRODUCTION

ROANOKE AND ITS GHOSTS

Roanoke today is a bustling center of commercial and cultural activity located in the southwest heart of Virginia. With a metropolitan area population of more than 300,000, the city is widely known as the "Capital of the Blue Ridge Mountains." Its history dates to the 1740s, when the first settlers arrived, attracted by large salt marshes, or "licks," that had drawn buffalo, elk, deer and Indians to the region for centuries. Consequently, the name given to the first settlement here was "Big Lick."

In the 1880s, the coming of the Shenandoah Valley Railroad triggered booming growth, and the town was renamed Roanoke, an Algonquin Indian word for shell or shell beads. The city has evolved into a center for transportation, distribution, trade, manufacturing, healthcare, entertainment, attractions and conventions. Two of these major attractions are a historic downtown marketplace where everything from fresh vegetables to fine art is sold and a one-hundred-foot-high steel, concrete and neon star atop Mill Mountain that has served as a homecoming beacon to generations of residents.

Roanoke may also be one of the most haunted cities in Virginia, if not the entire southeastern United States. Disembodied entities seem to abound here: in old mansions; on the grounds of long-abandoned plantations; in hotels, restaurants and bed-and-breakfast inns; in vintage theaters and ancient cemeteries; and even on local college campuses, where some buildings predate the Civil War.

This abundance of haunts has triggered a cottage industry. Each year, annual ghost walks are conducted in Roanoke, its sister city, Salem, and

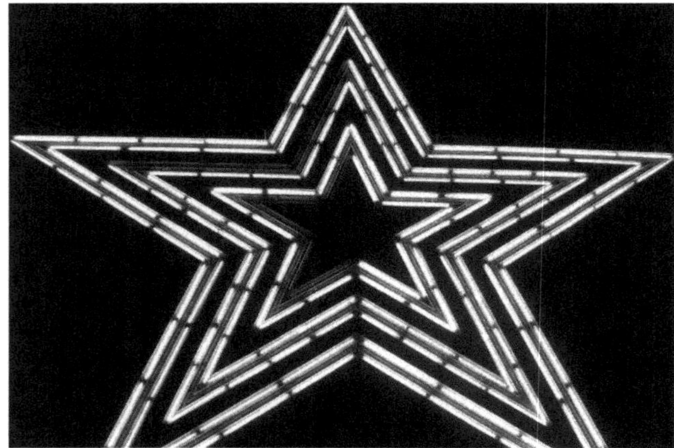

Left: The iconic one-hundred-foot star atop Mill Mountain has served as a beacon for Roanokers and visitors for generations. *Photo by C.J. Goens Jr.*

Below: The downtown historic Roanoke City Market has been a popular meeting place for Roanokers and visitors for more than a century. *Photo by Ruth Genter.*

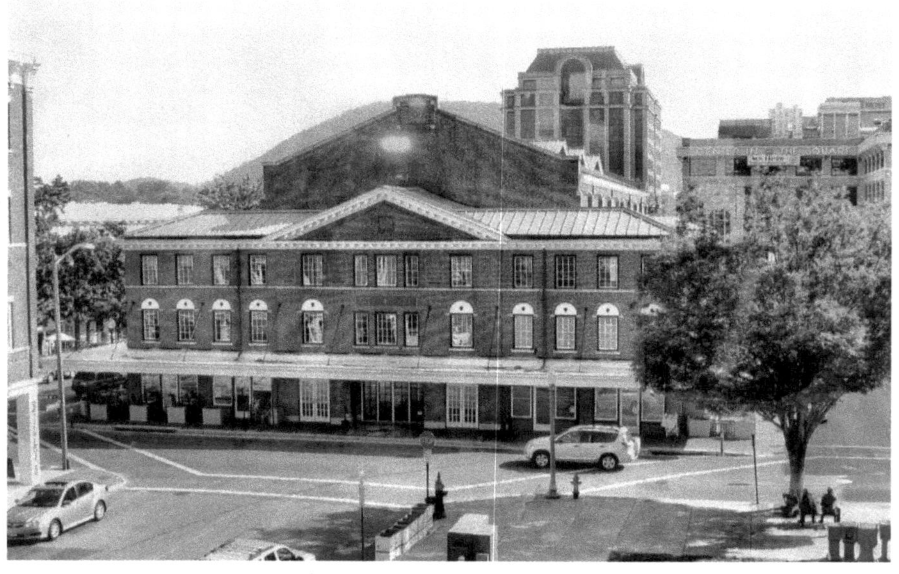

several surrounding communities. If the possibility of being scared by "real" spirits isn't enough, there is an assortment of haunted house attractions standing by, including the Fear Factory, Dark Forest and Dr. Pain's Nightmare, among others. Additionally, the high level of suspected paranormal activity in and around the city has led, in recent years, to the creation of a number of amateur ghost hunting groups. Their members are in general agreement: Roanoke is indeed a spooky place.

Roanoke's Phantom Woman in Black

She appeared out of nowhere. One witness "victim" described the unnerving experience like this: "It was as if she had arisen out of the earth." Her voice sounded real. Her touch felt real. She appeared to be real, although quite a few of the gentlemen involved had great difficulty looking her in the eye. A peripheral glance was the best some of them could manage in their fright. She never caused any physical harm, or at least none was reported. It seemed obvious at the time that for every man who summoned up enough courage to report her presence, there probably were three or four others who, for a variety of reasons, kept the mysterious meetings quiet.

Those who did look at her, and did come forward, were unanimous in at least one phase of her description: she was breathtakingly beautiful. One man said she was tall and handsome, with "dancing eyes." Another said she was about five feet, nine or ten inches tall, dressed entirely in black, "with something like a black turban on her head." It was, he added, fixed in such a manner so that it was drawn around her face just below her eyes, forming a perfect mask. She also wore a long black raglan cloak. "Her eyes," the man said, "were huge and her brows and lashes heavy, and if her forehead and eyes are proper index of that portion of her face concealed, she was very beautiful."

And then, in a flash, she would be gone. She would simply disappear, evaporate, vanish, leaving the men she escorted stunned and speechless. This was the legendary "Woman in Black," who, for a brief period in March 1902, struck terror into the hearts of the citizenry of Roanoke. The *Roanoke Times* reported, "Her name was on every lip; strong men trembled when her name was spoke;

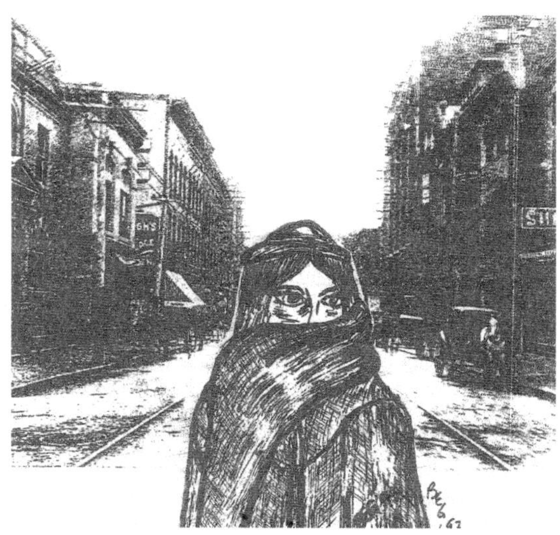

Roanoke's phantom "Woman in Black" terrorized the city for a brief period in 1902. *Illustration by Brenda E. Goens.*

children cried and clung to their mothers' dresses; terror reigned supreme!"

Who was this woman of dark intrigue, and what was her mission? Why was she so feared? As the newspaper pointed out, "Just why the Woman in Black should be so terrible has never been known. She made no attack on anyone. It was probably due to the unexpected appearance in places unthought of, and at hours when the last person of the city is expected about should be a woman."

She apparently had gone north from the city of Bristol, which, the *Times* reported, "is just recovering from the effects of the scare produced amongst the citizens of the town by what was known as the 'Woman in Black.' Hardly a day passed for weeks that the press of the town failed to have a long account of the antics and performance of the 'Woman in Black' on the night before." On March 18, 1902, the *Times* noted that

> *for the last ten days she has been unheard of; has completely disappeared from the city of Bristol; and expectation has been rife as to where she would make her next manifestation.*
>
> *More or less anxiety has been felt by a few people of Roanoke, who through necessity or otherwise are kept up until a late hour at night, lest she make her appearance before them; and true to the presentiment, to Roanoke she has come and in a quiet way is beginning to stir up some uneasiness and not a little excitement. Just what her mission here can be, what her object is in waylaying certain parties, has not exactly been figured out, but of one thing there seems to be a unanimity of opinion, and that is, she has a proclivity for attacking the married men, if "attack" is the proper word.*

The *Times* reported that there had been several recent encounters with the mystery woman. Here was one:

> *The most recent instance is that of a prominent merchant of the city, who, on the night after payday, having been detained at his store until after midnight, was making his way home, buried in mental abstractions, when at his side the woman in black suddenly appeared, calling him by his name. The woman was only a couple of feet behind him, and he naturally increased his pace; faster and faster he walked, but in spite of his efforts, the woman gained on him until, with the greatest of ease and without any apparent effort she kept along side of him. "Where do you turn off?" she asked of him. He replied in a hoarse voice, "Twelfth Avenue." Ere he was aware, she had hand upon his shoulder. He tried to shake it off, but without success. "You are not the first married man I have seen to his home this night," she spoke in a low and musical voice.*
>
> *Reaching the front gate, he made certain she would then leave him, but into the yard she went. This was a little more than he bargained for. It was bad enough to be brought home by a tall and handsome woman with dancing eyes, but to march up to the front door with her—well, he knew his wife was accustomed to wait for him when he was detained, and he did not dare to go to the trouble of making an explanation to her; besides, such explanations are not always satisfactory. The merchant admits that he was a nervy man, but that in spite of his efforts, he could not help being at least a little frightened. "Twas the suddenness of the thing," is the way he expressed it.*

But as he reached the door, he looked around. She was gone! Where she had gone, and how, he didn't know. But he didn't tarry on the doorstep either.

Two others who experienced these strange visitations were a porter and a young telegraph operator. Both were married, and in both cases, the woman appeared to them late at night on deserted streets. Each said that she moved over the sidewalk with an "almost noiseless tread." The porter was terrified by the apparition. He ran "two squares as fast as his legs could carry him" and "fell into the door almost in a fit." The telegraph operator said that she called out to him to "wait a minute," but like the porter, he ran hard all the way home. Both men later said that the woman had called them by name.

Whoever she was, she stayed in Roanoke only a short time. Within a few days, the reports of her appearances had ceased altogether. But soon there were accounts of her nightly sojourns in the town of Bluefield. Curiously, in that same month of March 1902, the *Roanoke Times* carried a short article from Alma, Nebraska. It was headlined, "Prominent Men See Ghost." The story noted, "The spirit form of a young woman is walking the streets of Alma. She exudes from the depths of some dark alley and rushes past lone pedestrians." One man said he saw "it" vanish in the moonlight, and another was chased by "it" after he scoffed at it. The dispatch added, "The Alma ghost is remarkable in that instead of being garbed in proverbial white, it walks about clothed in deep black."

Who was she? Why did she appear only to well-known married men, always late at night while they were on their way home? It has been speculated that perhaps she was a wife herself once who had found her husband unfaithful. Thereafter she returned to make sure potentially wayward males did not succumb to the temptations of the night.

Virginia's Most Haunted Hotel

It's no longer a hotel. The venerable building at 617 Jefferson Street in downtown Roanoke has been renovated, modernized and turned into luxury apartments, upscale offices and fancy restaurants. All this began in 2009 when a developer purchased the ailing, debt-ridden property and began a $20 million restoration. But for more than seventy years, this was the site of one of Virginia's most majestic and popular hotels: the Patrick Henry.

It first opened its doors to the public in 1925 and catered to the thousands of traveling salesmen who covered southwest Virginia. Upon entering the ornate, opulent lobby in years past, one got the feeling that he or she had somehow slipped into a time machine and been sent back to a scene of the 1920s. If ever a hotel in the commonwealth was remindful of the one depicted in the classic horror film *The Shining*, the Patrick Henry was it.

A glance around inside promoted the feeling that Jack Nicholson himself might materialize at any moment, complete with his flapper-era dinner jacket and slicked-black hair. It's not that such an entrance evoked chills; rather, it engendered a warm feeling of bygone elegance and the rich traditions of a time long past. In today's world of plastic motels, fast-food eateries and chain franchises, the Patrick Henry was a lone holdout of Victorian refinement and elegance, with all its attendant courtesies, politeness and class splendor. That's how it should be; that's how it was originally designed. The 117-room hotel opened to rave expectations, and for years, it was a sparkling showcase in regional circles of high society.

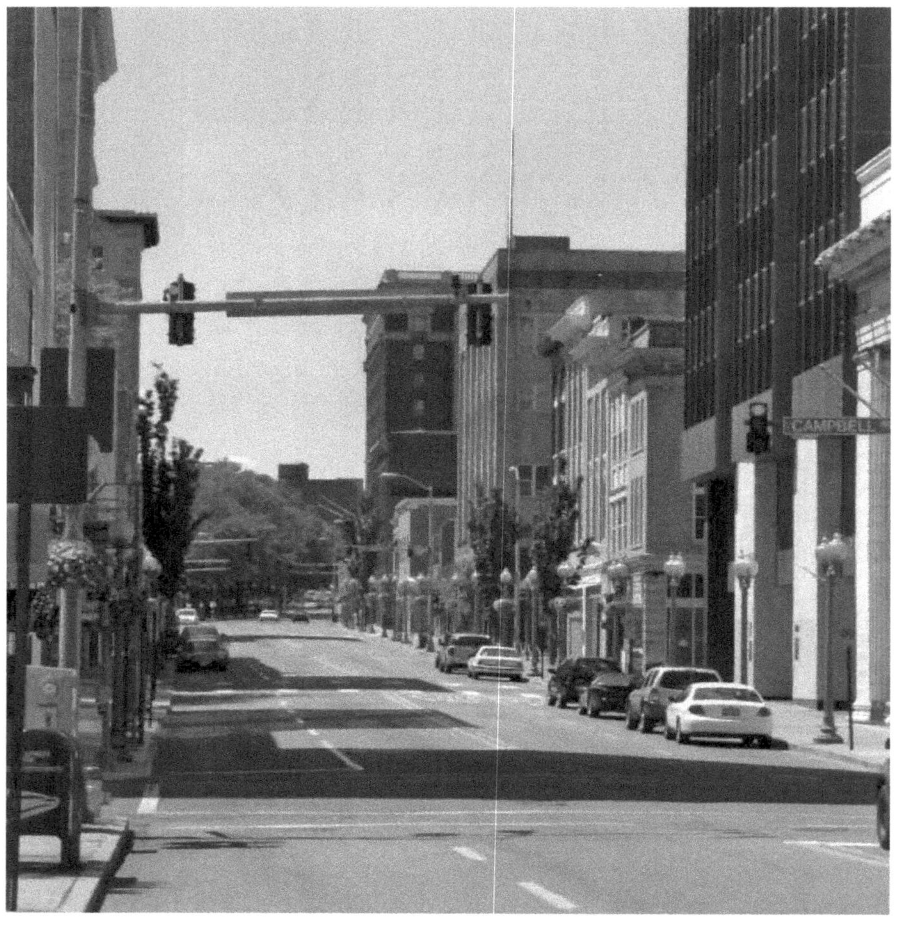

Street scene of downtown Roanoke. *Photo by Brenda E. Goens.*

In the 1930s, though, it fell victim to the Great Depression. To survive, its rooms were converted into apartments and, later, offices. Regrettably, its luxurious lobby was carved into cubicles, occupied by armies of clerks and stenographers. In 1991, however, new owners arrived and began renovations that brought it back to at least a close resemblance of its onetime magnificence. Elegant wrought-iron railings and accents of brass encircled the lobby. Ornate carvings embraced ceilings and walls. Beautiful chandeliers hung from ceilings that towered thirty feet overhead. But alas, these developers also fell on hard times, and the building stood abandoned for some time.

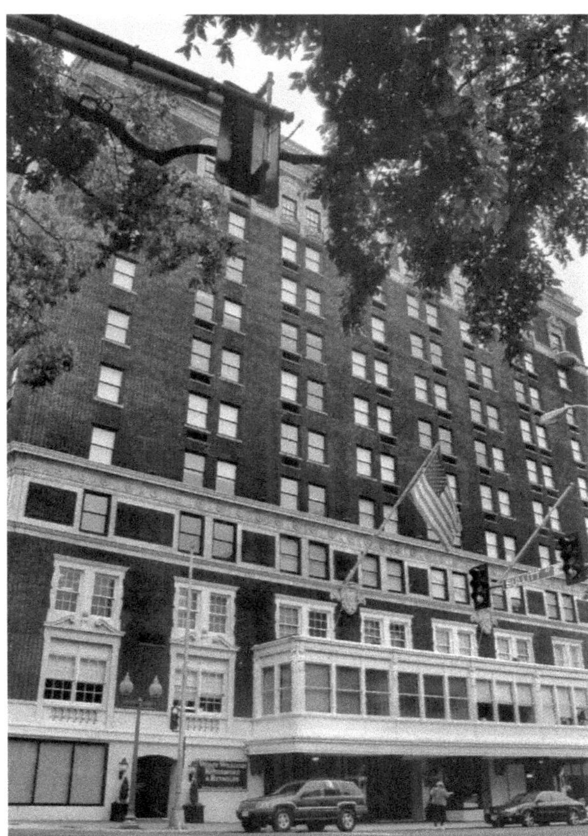

Right: Roanoke's Patrick Henry Hotel was, for decades, noted for its frequent paranormal activity. *Photo by Ruth Genter.*

Below: The lobby of the Patrick Henry Hotel was the site of unusual paranormal activity for decades. *Photo by the author.*

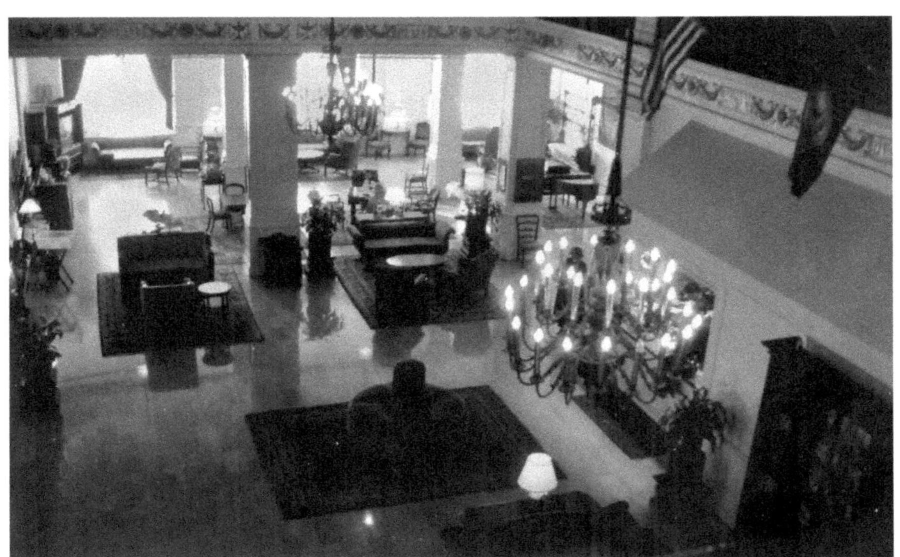

Under its new ownership, however, sincere efforts have been made to once again restore its original grandeur. The antique chandeliers have been painstakingly cleaned. The ballroom looks new, with replastered cornices and gleaming floors, and the old faux skylight above the atrium, which had been hidden by a newer ceiling, has been uncovered, adding a sense of space and light.

One thing that has not changed—something that the new residents, office workers and others may well soon discover—is the alleged fact that the old Patrick Henry is haunted. For decades, during its heydays and in between, there have been multiple reports of paranormal manifestations: lights inexplicably turned on and off, cold spots provoked shivers for those who walked through them and phantom footsteps were heard in darkened corridors.

In the latter days of the old hotel, groups of amateur ghost investigators set up their equipment here and rarely were disappointed. Gobs of orbs were seen flitting about on shots taken with digital cameras, and dozens of raspy, whispered EVPs (electronic voice phenomena) have been recorded, supposedly uttered by long-dead tenants. According to various reports these teams filed, three men dressed in tuxedos have been sighted in the ballroom. They vanished when approached. A predominant legend persists of an old lady named Lucy who long ago died in her room at the hotel but who still roams about at night in a long, flowing white gown. A former night auditor working late at the hotel one evening swore that he saw the apparition of a man dressed, like Nicholson, in clothes from the 1920s, standing on the terrace above the lobby. He also evaporated.

The most pronounced activity seems to center in what was once room 606 in the hotel. This was, in the early 1980s, the room where a young airline stewardess was brutally murdered. She was stabbed to death, and her bloodied body was stuffed into the bathtub. The killer was never found. In years afterward, room 606 became a hotbed of psychic phenomena.

According to former front office manager Doug Hall, the encounters peaked a few years later. "We had a woman guest staying in that room," he recalled in an interview with the author.

> *Suddenly, she showed up in the lobby late in the evening, dressed in her night clothes. She was obviously very upset. She said she had been asleep in her bed when she awoke and saw the ceiling above her open up. A spiral wrought iron staircase then descended from the opening, and a lady with dark hair, wearing a long black skirt with a magnolia blossom at the waist, a bonnet, and an old fashioned high collared blouse, came, down the*

staircase, glided over to the edge of the bed, and caressed the hair of the frightened guest. (In fact, there had been a staircase there years earlier, when the building had been converted into an apartment complex.)

"We offered to move the woman to another room," Hall continued, "but she steadfastly refused. She said there was no way she was going upstairs again after that. She spent the night in the lobby."

It is to room 606 that Deborah Carvelli used to take her students a few years ago when she taught parapsychology classes at Virginia Western Community College in Roanoke. A psychic, Carvelli and her students visited suspected area haunted sites to see what they could sense. She never told the class members the background history of the places they viewed. They went in ice cold. In room 606, Deborah turned out the lights and had everyone sit in the dark and concentrate.

Incredibly, some of the more intuitive students described the identical scene the female guest experienced. They visualized the ceiling open, the staircase descend and the apparitional woman come down the stairs. They accurately described her clothing as well. Carvelli said that the figure looked like the late Greek opera singer Maria Callas.

On a January night in 2002, the author accompanied Carvelli and one of her classes on a visit to room 606. The lights were turned off. There was a stony silence. Carvelli asked if anyone sensed anything. Again, no one had been told anything about what had happened in the room. Several students responded. Some were drawn to a closed closet door. "Someone was hiding in there," one said. They felt that a "major struggle" had occurred. Others were drawn to the bathroom and said that something terrible happened there. A few students said that they envisioned the bathtub being full of "blood and water." "Something is in here," one cried out. The intense atmosphere proved too oppressive for two of the students. They had to leave the room.

After everyone had volunteered what they had felt, Carvelli told them the facts of the case. She said that investigators had believed that the attacker had, in fact, hidden in the closet. After a fierce struggle, the girl was dead, and her body had been left in the bathtub. There was blood all over the bathroom. Some of the students said that they got the feeling that the victim knew her assailant. The police thought so, too.

Carvelli taught three each semester and said that students in each class had similar feelings about room 606. And despite the tragedy that took place there, former manager Doug Hall said that the room was often specifically requested by incoming guests. "I guess they had heard about it and had a keen interest in the paranormal," he surmised.

Whether one encountered a ghost or not at the Patrick Henry, the hotel, in its sunnier days, was well worth a visit, either as an overnight guest or just to walk through the sumptuous lobby and reminisce about the magnificence that once was.

Spirits Still Perking at the Coffee Pot

Motorists in southwest Virginia traveling north on state highway 221, as they enter Roanoke, suddenly come upon one of the most bizarre man-made sights in the state. To the uninitiated, it first comes as a shock, but this is quickly followed by sheer curiosity. What they see is a fifteen-foot-high wooden coffeepot on top of a locals-favorite roadhouse restaurant. The building has been a beloved fixture of the city for more than seventy-five years, and it is proudly listed as a Virginia historical landmark.

For the initiated, Roanoke natives, the Coffee Pot has long been and remains a favorite watering hole; here one can dine on homemade barbecue or southern fried chicken while listening to a broad range of down-home music provided by bands representing everything from jazz and bluegrass to country and blues, with an occasional appearance by a national star such as Richie Valens, Dickey Betts of the Allman Brothers or even Willie Nelson himself. And for an enticing encore, patrons may be treated to a ghostly manifestation or two; as the owner and staff members aver, fun-loving spirits lurk here.

Built in 1936 by Clifton and Irene Kefauver, the structure opened as a filling station and tearoom and soon after was converted into a restaurant. Architecturally, it is similar to a log cabin house topped by the towering coffeepot. For years, steam would rise from the pot's spout from a furnace located in the storeroom below, a welcoming beacon that could be seen for miles around.

Scores of bands, big and small, famous and obscure, have performed here over the years in what has been called "the biggest small stage in the

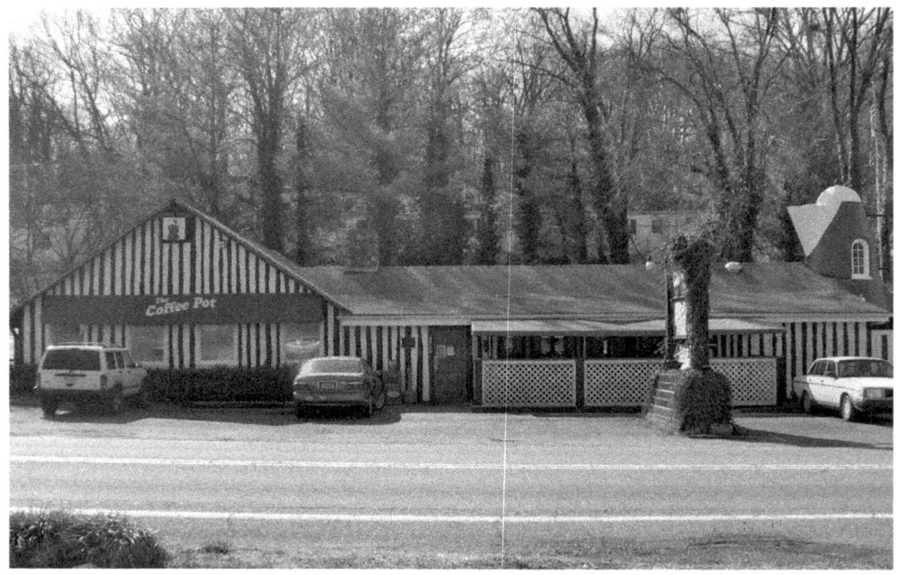

The city's colorful Coffee Pot restaurant, an iconic landmark for more than seventy-five years, is the site of mischievous ghostly activity. *Photo by Carol C. Goens.*

South." In the late 1970s, a surprise guest showed up here late one night. After singing to an audience of thousands at the Roanoke Civic Center, Willie Nelson appeared and gave a spontaneous encore to a thrilled group of local patrons. "I think he enjoyed the session more than his fans," said longtime owner Carroll Bell.

As to the paranormal activity, Bell, like many of his bartenders and servers, added, "We've got all kinds of ghosts. It's been interesting to say the least. I believe in spirits, and I'm convinced they are here. There are just too many strange incidents that occur to dismiss them all as coincidences." Bell, who has been owner here, off and on, for more than thirty-five years, said that both he and staff members have had personal encounters, usually when they are alone in the restaurant late at night.

"One bartender was here one night, washing ashtrays and stacking them up on a counter," Bell noted. "She said they suddenly rose up several inches in unison and then fell back down. No one else was in the room. When it happened a second time, she abruptly grabbed her coat and pocketbook and left. Another time, a worker heard a loud racket in the kitchen. She went in to look and saw a potholder, used to hold pot handles and spoons, swinging wildly. Again, no one else was around."

All sorts of unexplainable things seem to happen. One former manager said that stuff gets moved around on its own. Spices will turn up in unexpected places, and things will curiously disappear only to suddenly reappear elsewhere in plain view a day or two later. "Plastic wine bottles, full of wine, sometimes sail across a room, thrown by unseen hands," said Bell. "I was cooking one night when a package of fry powder flew out of the box on the shelf and smacked me in the middle of my back.

"One of the weirdest incidents happened one night when I was alone, closing up," Bell continued.

> *I went into the walk-in freezer, and the door slammed behind me. I heard the latch click shut, which had never happened before. The door doesn't automatically close. I said to myself, "Now what am I going to do?" I didn't have a cellphone with me, and the staff had all gone home. It's cold in here. I pushed against the door, but it wouldn't budge. I tried several times. Finally, in desperation, I walked back and few feet and then lunged forward as hard as I could, hitting the door with my shoulder. It flew wide open, and I went sprawling to the floor. It was like someone or something was playing a trick on me and had unexpectedly opened the latch.*

Bell believes that the ghosts are playful, not harmful. They seem to have a mischievous nature. Both he and his employees seem to think that the apparitional culprits may be either a former owner or a past cook, both of whom are deceased. "They loved the place," Bell said. "We figure they had an attachment to the Coffee Pot that somehow wasn't broken when they died. They're not scary. Whenever they act up, I just tell them to behave. It seems to work. Things usually quiet down after that. We've had paranormal investigators in here, and they confirm our beliefs. They've gotten all kinds of orbs with their cameras and inexplicable faint voices and whispers with their recording instruments."

Bell, who has tried to sell the restaurant several times, said, "I'll probably die with my hand taped to the draft beer tap, but come on in; I'll be glad to serve you. We have good food, great music, and who knows what else you might find."

Murder at the Mortician's Mansion

Roanoke native Carol Shepherd is a psychic, and psychics run in her family. When she was young, her father told her that she had such a gift—she could sense things others couldn't. She still does. She sees auras, or luminous radiations that surround people. She senses warnings. Once, she got a strong sensation that her cousin would be seriously injured or killed near water. When she learned soon afterward that he was going to Virginia Beach, she begged her mother to not let him go. He went anyway. At the beach, a storm brewed. As her cousin and two other boys were walking along the beach, lightning struck them. The two boys were killed. The bolt blew off the soles of her cousin's feet, and he was in a coma for some time, but he survived.

Several years ago, Carol had a near-death experience. Suffering from a severe brain fever, she envisioned herself leaving her body and being escorted across a marble bridge. Across the water, she saw her friends and relatives who had passed on. Just before reaching the other side, she was told that they were not yet ready for her; she still had work to do on earth. She was returned.

Carol worked for years as a rescue volunteer. She and many others at the East Hanover Rescue Squad in Mechanicsville, Virginia, experienced a number of paranormal events in their building. Inexplicable noises were heard, blue lights flashed through the place at times and once, for a fleeting few seconds, the face of an African American man crying was seen in a window. It was later learned that the building had been built over an old cemetery for blacks.

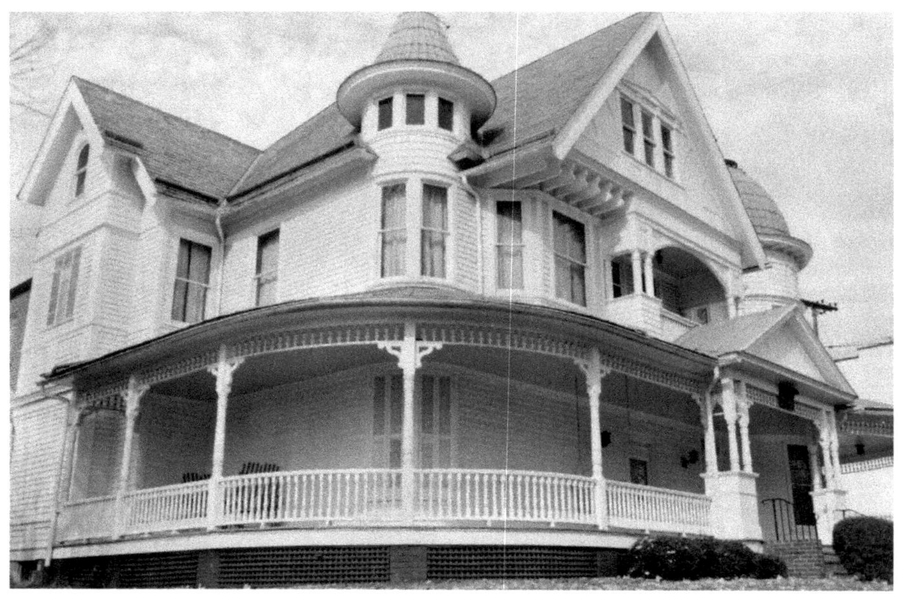

The mortician's mansion on Patterson Avenue, SW, no longer standing, was the scene of mystery, intrigue and possible murder. *Photo by the author.*

The most chilling experience Carol has encountered occurred at an old house in Roanoke when she was a young girl, about eight years old. She was not the only one who was a witness. Others, both children and adults, also attested to the weird happenings that eventually led to the discovery of a dark tragedy. This is how she remembers it:

> *It was a big house in the 1100 block of Patterson Avenue in the southwestern section of the city. There were three stories. It had turrets and gables and a big wraparound porch. I think it dated to the 1880s. There was a vacant lot next to it and a big rock wall around it. I guess you could say it was a spooky house, but we played around it all the time in the daytime and never really thought about it. What I remember best was a playhouse that had been built for the children there. Of course, they weren't there when I was growing up. They had been gone for years. It was around 1950 or so when I remember playing there.*
>
> *I didn't know much about the house then. We had heard it was a mortician's house and that a family had once lived there: a man, his wife and four children. But that had been a long time ago. We used to play around the place all the time. Looking back on it, I guess there were some*

very strange things happening, but as kids, we didn't think much about it. It had been vacant a long time. Every once in a while, some people would move in, but they always moved right back out within a few days or weeks. No one stayed in the house very long. It was such a pretty house, it wasn't hard to get people to move in, but it was sure hard to keep them there.

In retrospect, I guess we should have been scared about some of the things that went on, but we were too young to realize how frightening it was. I mean, for example, when the house had been vacant for some time, we would see things in it. At night, sometimes you could see blue lights flashing inside. It had once been a funeral home. The man must have used the first floor for his funeral parlor and the basement for his work in preparing the deceased for burial. The basement had a dirt floor. The family lived on the upper floor.

My sister reminded me that we saw what appeared to be a body on a gurney with a sheet over it. She said the sheet moved up and down, like someone was breathing underneath it. We would see windows in the attic open and shut, but we didn't think about the fact that no one was in the house. If we had, I guess we would have been scared. One thing that did frighten us was that we occasionally would see what looked like a cat with red shining eyes inside the house.

And then there was the woman. We would see a woman in the house. Sometimes she would be standing at a window upstairs, watching us play. It never really dawned on us at the time that there was no one in the house. She would always be dressed in a long, flowing white gown, kind of like a nightgown. The gown was yoked at the top and had long sleeves. She had beautiful blonde hair. She would just look down at us and smile. Sometimes, if you looked through her windows, you could see her on the stairs. Back then, we had no idea of who she was or why she was there. She was pretty, and I would say she was in her mid-thirties.

Other times, I would babysit for the people who lived next door, and we would see lights going on and off in the house at night. This was strange because the electricity had been cut off. You could hear doors slamming and people yelling inside. We heard screams a few times.

I didn't learn 'til later the story about the people who had once lived there—the mortician, his wife and four children. Years ago, the woman and the children disappeared. The man said they had gone to visit relatives, but they never returned. Then, about two years later, he disappeared. I would hear my parents and other adults talk about this. They would talk about the people who later moved in and moved right out again. They said mysterious things happened there. Apparently, there were a lot of dark rumors floating around the neighborhood about the house.

Well, when we told my father about the lady we had seen in the house, and he knew there shouldn't be anybody there, it aroused his curiosity. So, one day, he and another man went over to the house. It had been abandoned for some time. The doors were locked, but they forced open a door and went inside through the back of the house. My father went up what he said was a very narrow staircase to the second floor. And then he saw her! He saw the woman in the white gown. She was looking out a window. He said she turned and smiled at him and then dematerialized right in front of him. He quickly got out of there.

He later said he didn't understand her appearance at all because there was about a two- or three-inch layer of dust throughout the house, yet there were no footprints anywhere. I think he was pretty shaken by the experience because he went to the sheriff, who was a friend of his, and told him they had better investigate the place. He told the sheriff to bring a long rod to poke around.

They found five bodies in the basement buried under the dirt floor. They suspected it was the wife and children of the mortician. They also found a number of graves in the yard around the house. All I remember was that we were told we couldn't play near the house anymore. Later, they tore the house down, and I understand the city wouldn't let anybody build anything there. Some years later, I visited Roanoke and drove out to the site, and all that was there was the old rock wall. Everything else was gone. As far as I know, they never did find out where the mortician went. He was never heard from again.

One puzzle was unraveled, however: the cat with the gleaming eyes. It turned out to be a ceramic cat. It had ruby red eyes. I guess the reflection of light made them seem to shine. They found some old caskets in the basement, and a gurney with a sheet over it like the one we had seen.

But the mystery of the woman who stood in the window and watched us play has never been solved. Who was she? Was she the mortician's wife who came back searching for her children? And what unspeakable horror of so many years ago could she describe? I guess we'll never know.

The Paranormal Wedding Dress

Was it a premonition or just plain coincidence? Whatever the case, it was highly unusual, to say the least, and it surely qualifies to fall within the shadowy realm of the unknown. The experience was told anonymously by a Roanoke woman on the Internet a few years ago and was reported in area newspapers.

About thirty-five years ago, the woman was moving from her house to an apartment. She was leaving her second husband. Her first marriage, to her high school sweetheart, had ended tragically after five years when he was killed in an auto accident. Some of her items were left by mistake in her second husband's house, including her first wedding dress, which she prized. She went back to retrieve them several times but was unsuccessful in that no one would ever answer the door.

Fast-forward about thirty years. "One Friday," she said, "I was dusting and I happened to look up at a picture of me in that wedding dress, and I was thinking about the dress and how wonderful it would be to have it for my granddaughters. The following Monday, I decided to paint some chairs, but had to go to the hardware store to get some paint."

She got in the car, and instead of turning left to the paint store, for some unexplained reason, she turned right. She then thought that as long as she was heading that way, she would go to a fabric store in that direction for some material to cover the chairs. But instead of parking in front of the fabric store, she pulled in at the other end of a mall—again without consciously knowing why—and then asked herself what she had done that for.

So, she began the long walk to the other end of the mall. "As I did," she said, "I passed an antique consignment shop that I had never been in. I decided to go in there. I went in and turned to the right and was looking at some things, alone, when I heard a voice say, 'Go in the back!' I instinctively turned and went in the back. I looked up, and someone had a little booth with a louvered door, and on that door was a dress—my wedding dress!"

"I was so stunned, I started shaking. I ran and got the clerk. I told her to get the dress down because I wanted to buy it. She asked if I didn't want to know how much it cost, and I said I didn't care," she continued. "The clerk asked how I knew it was mine, and I told her to look inside and she would see a label. It came from Lazerus, an old dress shop in downtown Roanoke. I knew it was mine because when we bought it, it was one of a kind. Isn't that wild? It's the wildest thing that ever happened to me. I believe there is no such thing as coincidence. I was led there! Even though he [her first husband] has been dead all these years, you just never forget."

When the woman posted her experience on the Internet, another woman responded, "You are right. It was no coincidence. We are guided every day of our lives, although at times we may not realize it, and at other times, like your case, we know we had help. With all the rush in the world today, most of us do not stop to listen."

HOME BUT NOT ALONE

Variations of the following account have appeared on the Internet's myriad ghost sites from time to time. The original source of the material was found among stacks of English students' papers on the subject of the paranormal at Radford University. One involved an interview with a woman from Salem (Roanoke's adjacent sister city) named Nebra Crockett, and it is excerpted here with permission of Radford University.

Mrs. Crockett said that when her family moved into the "drafty old house" in the 1980s, they had been told that the place was haunted; that strange things happened there. It was said that previous occupants had what were called "running fits"; that tenants would sometimes race out of the house in the dead of night for no apparent reason. The Crocketts were also told that no one had lived there for any length of time. Renters would move in and then suddenly move out again, and the house would often stand empty.

When the family entered it, Mrs. Crockett said she felt cold spots, even in the summer, but she attributed it to the draftiness of an old structure. She also felt "motion" at times, as if someone or something was passing by her. "A lot of times," she said, "you could walk into a room and you'd get the feeling that there was something else besides you there, but I just thought it was my imagination, and I didn't think too much about it." But then, as more curious incidents unfolded, she began to change her mind.

"When my first girl was born, I nursed her," Mrs. Crockett continued. "It was always my practice to stay up to midnight to take care of the baby and the 12 o'clock feeding. Usually, my husband would get up and give me the baby at two a.m., and I would nurse her in bed, and just let her stay in bed with me until the next morning. Well, one night, I believe it was in October, my husband had a cold and had taken some medication before going to bed.

"I was asleep when someone began shaking me on my shoulder. The baby was crying. I thought it was my husband, but I looked over and he was sound asleep. All of a sudden I realized that someone else was there. I looked up, and there was a little old lady standing over me and she had me by the shoulders and was still shaking me. It scared me to death! I sat up straight and reached out for her...and she was gone! So I got up, got the baby, and went back to bed and nursed her. Then I put her back in her crib and when I got back to bed, it was like cold ice water all over. I was shaking. I was so scared. But I didn't tell anyone about it then.

"Several days later, I was making up the bed and I felt a presence. I just told 'her' that this was my home now and I intended to stay here. 'She' wasn't going to run me off. She apparently had run other people off, but I was staying and that was it. I felt like a fool, but that was all right. I meant what I said. And after that I didn't feel any recurrence of the presence for a long time."

Mrs. Crockett went on: "The next odd thing took place on a Christmas Eve. We had bought a dining room suite, and we were going down to the store to pay for it and bring it home. When we all went together, I would call the roll of the children to make sure everyone was in the car: Lara, Luella, Latisha, Sam, Edgar, and the baby, Mary. Everyone was there. Then the phone rang in the house and I had to go back in. Edgar was only three at the time, and since there was snow on the ground, he decided he would go back into the house to get his boots. I didn't know he had done this.

"So when I got back in the car, I didn't think anything about it, because Edgar would often crawl up in the back of the seat and go to sleep. I just assumed he had done this. After we had driven for awhile, I said to Lara, 'Edgar's awful quiet. Is he asleep? And she said. 'Mama, Edgar's not in the car!'

"So we made a U turn, and my imagination ran wild. I could imagine him crying out in the snow. I could visualize him pulling over a heavy piece of furniture on top of him. I imagined everything. When we got back to the house, there was not a sound. He wasn't out in the street, he wasn't on the porch, and I couldn't find him in the house. He wasn't crying. I was frantic that something had happened to him. I called out, 'Edgar, where are you?' And finally I heard him: 'Mama, I'm in the library.'

"I ran into the library and he was sitting on the couch and he had three little cards that he'd been drawing on. I said, 'Aren't you glad to see me?

Weren't you scared? Weren't you upset when we left you?' He said no, and when I asked him why, he said 'the little old lady came. As soon as you left she was here and she said for me not to cry, and she gave me these cards to draw on.'

"I asked Edgar where the woman was now, and he said, 'As soon as you opened the door, she left.' Then I asked him what she looked like, and he said she looked like grandma, 'she's a little old lady like grandma,' and that was all I ever got out of him."

Sometime later, the Crocketts were shown an old photograph of the house, which was believed to date to the 1830s. Standing in front of the house in the picture was an old woman who had been identified as "Mrs. Anderson," who lived there long ago. When Mrs. Crockett saw the photo, she gasped.

"I know the little old lady who stood over me at my bedside was the same little old lady that was in the picture," she exclaimed. "Because her hair was slicked back and she had piercing features, her nose and her eyes and all. She was just as real as you are real at that particular moment, and then it was 'poof,' and she was gone!" Edgar, too, identified the woman in the picture as the same woman who had calmed him the day he had been left behind in the house.

"I felt she was there to help," Mrs. Crockett said. "She came to let me know my baby was crying and needed to be fed, and she was there to take care of Edgar when he was home alone."

Recollections of a Psychic Family

Is it possible for an entire family to be psychically sensitive? One begins to wonder after talking to Mary Vaught of Roanoke. She and her brothers and sisters seemingly are able to recite ghostly incident after incident, all different, depending on with whom you are talking. And that can add up to a lot of incidents because at one time there were fifteen children in the family, ten girls and five boys. Strange things just seemed to happen to them all.

The paranormal inheritance might stem from Mary's late mother, Annie Hope Tillet. She was born in 1912, and according to her children, she was a true psychic. "She used to tell me when I was real little that you should never be afraid of ghosts," said Alma Heixenbaugh, one of Mary's sisters. Alma added that when she was six years old, "My mother told me that she would die when I was fifteen. She said that everyone had a time to die, and she knew when hers was. And she did. She died when I was fifteen. She had come home from the hospital for Thanksgiving, and she told us, 'You'd better give me my Christmas presents now, because I won't be around for Christmas.' She died that night!"

Alma had another psychic revelation in March 1996. She dreamed one night of seeing a man riding a pale horse. "He was riding toward my brother and mother, but I couldn't see his face," she said. Her father died shortly after the dream.

Mary Vought has had strange experiences, too. The strongest occurred when she and her husband, Carter, and their children moved into a house at 1232 Kerns Avenue in Roanoke in 1963. "I could sense the house was haunted," Mary said.

> *I got sick right after we moved in, and we went to one doctor after another, but they couldn't determine what was making me sick. I think it was the house.*
>
> *We used to hear the door knob turning at night, and then someone or something coming up the stairs. We all heard it. We would hear moans. One time our son, Carter Jr., said something unseen pushed him into a closet and then locked the door. At first, my husband was a skeptic, but in time he began to believe. He said one night he was sitting on the bed in our bedroom upstairs playing the guitar at about six in the evening. The children were all outside playing. He said he heard someone coming up the stairs. He knew it wasn't any one of us. Then he saw the door knob to the room turning and the door starting to open. He got off the bed, went over to the door and raised the guitar over his head. When he opened the door, he swung the guitar down to bash whoever it was over the head, but he said the guitar just swished air. There was no one there!*

On another occasion, Mary's daughter, Marylyn, was in her bed one night when she saw the shadowy vision of an old farmer in old-timey clothes. He stood at the end of her bed. She hid under the covers, and when she finally peeked out, the apparition was gone.

"A lot of things happened in that house," Mary added. "Another time, I couldn't get the front door to open, and a neighbor came over to help me. There was no one in the house, but we both heard someone running up the stairs and the door slamming. She grabbed a baseball bat, and we looked all over, but we didn't find anything." Mary said that no one could live in the house for more than a few months before moving out. "We finally had to get out of that house, and as soon as we did, I wasn't sick anymore."

But her encounters weren't limited to the place on Kerns Avenue. Once she was sitting on a porch at another house, just outside Salem. "The moon was real bright that night, and everything was so quiet and still," she remembered. "The next thing I knew, I looked up and saw a man with a khaki shirt and khaki pants, and he walked right towards me. I said, 'Who are you? Get out of here!' And when my husband turned on the lights, he had vanished in thin air! I know the bedroom we slept in would get icy cold at times, even in summer, and sometimes you could smell roses when there weren't any flowers in the house; I mean a real strong scent, like you were in a funeral home."

She continued: "That area was really haunted. You could knock on the door of just about any house there, and people would tell you a hair-raising story or two. There was a legend that a young couple jumped off the railroad trestle because they were too young and couldn't get married. They were killed, but people said you could still see their spirits there on certain nights."

Apparently, the psychic sensitivities of the family are being passed on, generation after generation. Annie Hope Tillet seems to have given them to her children. And now, said Alma Heixenbaugh, Mary's sister, her daughter may have inherited the "second sight." Alma said that when her daughter was thirteen, she envisioned Alma having an auto accident…the day before she had one.

CONVERSATIONS WITH A DEAD MAN

Kathy Firebaugh of Roanoke thinks she is a sensitive. "All my life I've been very perceptive," she said. "It's like I see things—flashes of things in advance sometimes. Things zip through my head. Like when someone dies, I may get a flash vision of it. I'm somehow predisposed to these types of feelings. Maybe I'm psychically sensitive. I don't know. It can be a scary thing, and when I feel a premonition of something bad, I try to put it out of my mind. But often what I sense happens soon after."

Kathy's paranormal "abilities," if that's what they are, were put to the test a few years ago in a series of encounters with her father-in-law, Ralph, both when he was alive and after he had passed on. Here's how she described it:

> *He and I were always very close. I called him Dad. We had a lot of long talks, and he always confided in me. We had a special bond. When he got sick, he had a weak heart, I would visit him a lot, both at his home and at the hospital. He seemed concerned about what would happen to his wife if he died, and he asked me to look after her. He also was concerned about Tommy, his son and my husband. We talked about him a lot.*
>
> *I knew in advance when I got a call late one night that it was about Dad—that something had happened to him. I was right. He had died. Sometime later, we decided to take my mother-in-law, Alice, to the beach. We stayed at an ocean-side motel. One day, I went out of the room to smoke a cigarette. I was just standing there, alone, when it happened.*

Dad spoke to me! His voice was clear, loud and strong. There was no mistaking it either. It definitely was the voice of my late father-in-law. I can't remember his exact words, but he asked me how his wife was. I was stunned. It scared me so bad. I immediately turned a full circle, looking all around for a visible source for the voice, but there was none. No one was anywhere near. I started shaking all over. I was freezing, and it was crazy because it was warm. This was the middle of summer.

Dad went on. He told me Alice worried him. She was going too far out in the water on a raft. He told me to keep an eye on her. All this time, he was talking in a very conversational, though a little loud, tone, like it was a natural thing to him. He didn't seem to realize the effect it was having on me. He asked about Tommy and how he was doing. He seemed to be listening and taking in my responses.

Then he left. I couldn't see him, but I knew somehow that he was leaving. I could feel his presence leaving. And then the most miraculous thing happened. I saw this grand image. I saw a vision of Dad. He was walking across a field. I could see his face clearly. It was definitely him. There were other people in the background, in the field. They all seemed to be very happy. They had musical instruments, and they were singing.

There is no earthly way to describe what I saw. It was something on a different plane, something I had never experienced before. It was the most beautiful scene I had ever seen. I can't describe the depth of colors I saw. There were colors we don't have here on earth. And Dad was there, and he seemed to be contented. It was a peaceful scene. It was heavenly.

And then the vision disappeared. I sat there sobbing and shaking. It was an overwhelming experience for me. I thought for a minute that I was losing my mind. I was too scared to tell anybody about it for a long time. I wouldn't even talk about it with Tommy. Afterwards, there were times when I would find myself crying. I was frightened, though I knew the whole thing was not threatening to me in any way. It was just overpowering.

As time went on, her father-in-law made periodic visits to Kathy, but he never reappeared in visual form. It was always his voice that she heard:

Usually, he comes back to see how his wife is doing and how Tommy is. I remember one specific time. Tommy's mom gave us an old accordion that had belonged to Dad. He was very musically inclined. The accordion had a broken strap, and we were having a very difficult time trying to find a replacement strap. We had looked everywhere, but as the instrument was old, we couldn't find a strap.

Well, one day Dad appeared, or at least I heard his voice. Clearly, he told me to go to Happy's. This was an out-of-the-way flea market in north Roanoke. Then he gave me directions. He said go all the way back to the end of the market and turn left, and there, we would find a strap for the accordion. Again, I thought I was losing it. Nevertheless, we went to Happy's, and I led the way to the end of the aisle and turned left, and there was a booth that carried musical equipment. I couldn't believe it. They didn't have the accordion strap, but they said they normally carried it, and if we came back, they would have one for us.

Over the next three years, Kathy was visited by Dad about a dozen times. Each time, he asked about his wife and other members of the family. "It's like a bolt of lightning in your thought process," Kathy said. "He used me as a conduit. I guess I'm somehow sensitive. Sometimes he told me where to look for certain papers his wife needed. The papers were always right there where he directed me. I had no doubt that if a question arose, about his will, his estate, his business papers or anything else, he would tell me what to do. I think he is there—here—to look out for his wife. He knew that she trusted me and that I would help take care of her. That's why I think his spirit lingered here."

One day, when Tommy had taken part in a musical program at church, Dad visited Kathy once again. "I had left the service early and had gotten into the car when I heard his voice once more," Kathy said. "He told me he was excited that Tommy was showing an interest in music. He had always encouraged Tommy in this way. He said it was about time Tommy started doing that. I smiled…I think Dad is at peace now."

The Sad Ghosts of the Grandin Theatre

Saturday, March 26, 1932, was a banner day for the citizens of Roanoke. That was the date the majestic Grandin Theatre, the first one in the city exclusively wired for sound movies, opened its doors, following a police-escorted parade through downtown. Admission was twenty-five cents for adults and fifteen cents for children. The first picture shown was *Arrowsmith*, starring Ronald Coleman and Helen Hayes. The theater became the centerpiece of Grandin Village, an eclectic district now listed on the National Register of Historic Places.

Today, while nearly a dozen other "golden era" theaters have succumbed to the vagaries of time, the Grandin—along the district, dotted with independently owned retail and dining establishments—has flourished. It wasn't always that way, however. There is, in fact, a long and checkered history. In 1976, for example, the entertainment house had to be shut down, deep in debt. Then fate stepped in. The Mill Mountain Theater was destroyed by fire, and its players moved into the Grandin. That lasted seven years, after which the doors were closed again. A local entrepreneur stepped in to the rescue, and for two years, the Grandin became both a movie house and a concert hall. Such renowned artists as Ray Charles, B.B. King and Dave Brubeck performed to capacity audiences.

Alas, the theater's lights were darkened once more due to the failure to pay power bills. It reopened a year later, hosting movies, art exhibits and live concerts, but in 2001, financial problems again set in, and the stage and screen were mothballed one more time. A year later, a group of leading

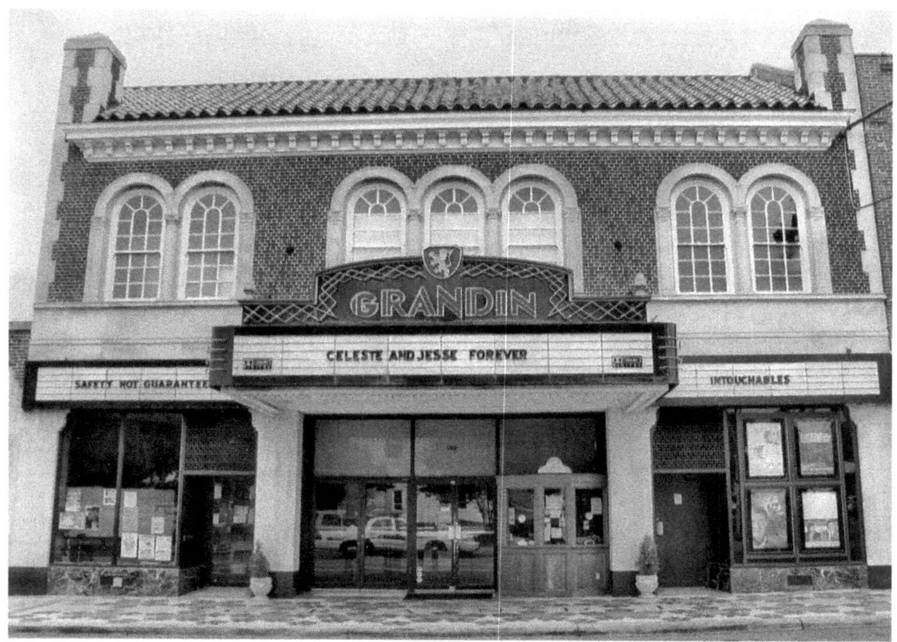

The Grandin Theatre has been a celebrated Roanoke landmark for more than eighty years and is known for its first-run movies and resident ghosts. *Photo by Ruth Genter.*

citizens formed the Grandin Theatre Foundation, raised money and then renovated and reopened the venerable building. Today, the apparently unsinkable house is a popular meeting place featuring the finest in first-run, foreign, documentary, independent and children's films.

It also is allegedly haunted. In a legend that has survived from generation to generation, it is believed that a homeless family made their home in the projection booth during one of the times the theater was closed. Supposedly, two of their children died during their stay, either from exposure or sickness. The psychic phenomena includes Grandin employees hearing the unexplained sounds of a phantom baby crying after the place had reopened, as well as eyewitness accounts of the sighting of a strange man staring down from the projection booth above. At other times, when the house was otherwise deserted, workers heard what they described as the sounds of a party going on, including laughter and clinking glasses.

The most chilling episode took place one night after the theater had closed for the evening. A member of the cleanup crew saw a small boy at the top of a stairwell. Thinking that the youngster somehow had been left behind, the employee went up the stairs. He said the child then flatly disappeared by walking *through* a screening room door.

In recent years, a number of local and regional amateur ghost hunters have set up their sensitive gear and investigated the Grandin after it had closed to the public for the night. They have not been disappointed, finding a variety of orbs on their digital camera pictures and faint yet unmistakable whispered voices on their EVP equipment.

EMBODIMENTS OF EVIL

The following two accounts, about houses in Roanoke, were submitted to me separately by two young women unknown to each other, yet their narratives are strikingly similar to the nature of the phenomena and in the intense fear they engendered. Cathy Webb wrote that while she didn't consider herself psychic, "I am convinced that I saw something that was the embodiment of evil." Here, excerpted, is her report.

I was born in Roanoke. In 1954, my parents found a stately, white brick colonial that had been built in the 1930s, for sale in North Roanoke on Collingwood Street. Although I was only three at the time, the house and its lot remain vivid in my memory. Painted white brick with black shutters, the house was situated on a large lot bisected in the rear by a little brook. More than 50 rose bushes surrounded the flagstone patio. Inside, cedar-lined closets and stone fireplaces on two levels were featured. Because the house was so large for just the three of us, my mother's parents moved in with us and took over the master suite upstairs.

Despite the sedate beauty of the house and its environs, there was an underlying, sinister pulse of negative energy that I sensed even as a toddler. My parents purchased the home from the estate of a family who had all died in an accident. As we settled in, I began to fear certain parts of the house, even in broad daylight; the fear of certain closets, stairways, and the attic seemed pronounced.

After our first month there, things began to go wrong. While my father mowed the lawn one day, the bolt that held the mower blade in place sheared off, sending the blade flying across the lawn like some medieval weapon. Days later, I was swinging on a rope string tied to a willow tree in the backyard. Suddenly, the rope snapped and I sailed into a thorny rose bush. It appeared as if someone had cut halfway through the rope! Later, when my parents got into a heated argument, the lights went out for no reason. Another time my mother was upstairs in the bath, alone, when a bat flew in and frightened her to the point of fainting. As such incidents mounted, so did the tension in our family.

After I turned four, I was with my grandparents in their room one night. There is a door there that leads to the attic, and they warned me never to open it. I disobeyed. To this day, I clearly remember what I saw staring at me from the top of the attic stairs. There was something not quite human staring down at me! Dressed in gray work pants with a plaid flannel shirt and suspenders, was what appeared to be a wizened old man with a wrinkled face, tufts of clownish red hair sticking out from a balding pate, and exposing a bloody red maw.

Where eyes should have been were two dark empty sockets. I began screaming, and I suppose someone must have shut the attic door, but I remember very little else, save for the recurring nightmares of the horrible image. Despite my age, I knew whatever I had seen was demonic and no doubt part of the house. Not long after this incident, my parents separated and we moved away.

As I later learned, other families encountered this malefic presence. The couple that bought the house from us also divorced within a year of moving in, and death claimed the father of the next family who moved in after them. Then, in the fall of 1969, while I was in college, my mother called me and said the house we had lived in on Collingwood Street was listed for sale. Despite all that had happened to us there, my mom had always adored the house. She was interested, but after viewing the place, she heard nothing from the owner. Later, she learned that the owner had died alone in the master bedroom, where I had seen the "demon." There was no apparent cause of death. The woman had appeared to be perfectly healthy. Her passing had gone undiscovered for days.

Long after I had moved out of town, in 1999, I was back in Roanoke on a business trip, and, on a whim, decided to go by the old house. I asked the present owner if it was still haunted. "Yes," she replied. "There was a hateful presence in the house for the first two years we lived here," she added. "The house had been vacant for a long time after the mysterious death of the owner in 1969. In fact, a number of the neighbors had begged me not to buy it, describing it as cursed, haunted, you name it. I soon found out what they meant."

She believed that stark fear had played a part in the death of the previous owner. Neighbors told her that the immediate previous family to live there was so terrified of the house that they burned candles in almost every room around the clock. I then asked her how she had managed to stay there, in a place so full of tragedy and sorrow. She said, "I told that hateful thing, whatever it was, that this was my house and to stay away from me and my children. 'He' kept his distance for years, and then one evening there was an unexplained fire in the chimney. After that, I knew he was gone. I haven't been bothered since then."

Webb concluded that she had a hunch that someone had been murdered in the house before or just after it was completed in the 1930s. She closed her letter with this: "Despite the passing of many years and coming to terms with my childish nightmares, there are nights that I recall, unbidden, the horrible image, and, frightened as I was so long ago, I will rush to turn on the bedside light to rid myself of that gruesome memory. Even now, remembering the demon, I will sleep with the lights on!"

This second account was submitted by a young woman who, for privacy reasons, identified herself only as "Marilyn."

There are some things in my life that have truly terrified me, things that I could never explain. When my parents rented the big two-story house on Kerns Avenue in Roanoke, I was tickled to death. This soon changed once we came to realize that the house was haunted!

It was a huge three bedroom house. It was November 1967 when we moved in. I shared a bedroom with my two younger sisters. I took the bed nearest a walk-in closet. Big mistake! We all noticed a stain on the hardwood floor the day we moved in, but my dad installed hardwood floors and he sanded the stain out. Houses like this were usually out of our price range, but not this one. The rent was only $60 a month, far below the going rate for a place like this.

Strange things began almost immediately. My parents heard footsteps of someone coming up the stairs. They stopped right outside their bedroom, but when dad checked, there was no one there. Then one night in December, an event occurred which terrified me. My sisters were asleep, and I laid there, awake. I began to hear a faint sound of musical notes being played. It became louder. The sounds seemed to be coming from the closet beside my bed. Chills ran down my spine. It sounded like someone was plucking on nails that were sticking out of the wall. I bolted out of bed and ran downstairs to my parents. I was crying hysterically. They went up with me to check out the closet. But now the room was silent. They tried to convince me I had been dreaming, but I knew the difference between a dream and reality. As soon as they left and I was about to drift off to sleep, the musical nails sound began again. This time I screamed! My parents then had me switch beds with one of my sisters.

A few nights later, my brother, who slept in a separate bedroom, heard a soft moaning sound coming from his closet. Then he heard his matchbox car collection crash to the floor, as if hurled by some unseen force. No one was in the room with him. We then started asking the neighborhood kids if they had heard anything strange about the house, and they told us a man had died in my brother's bedroom from a brain tumor.

Soon thereafter, I had my own ghostly encounter. In the middle of the night I was awakened with the distinct feeling that I was being watched. I looked over at the doorway, and stared straight at terror! There stood something looking in at me. The person, if indeed it was a person, was dressed in an old, flowing, dark hooded robe. I had the feeling I was looking at something that was pure evil! I ducked my head under the covers, and when I peeked out later, it was gone. The next morning I asked mom if she had come to check on us during the night. She said that neither she nor dad had gotten up.

Things got worse. My parents were continuously awakened by the footsteps coming up the stairs at night. My dad said he felt coldness pass over him as the footfalls made their way up to the landing where he stood watch. Then the stain he had sanded off the floor—returned. It looked like a blood stain. Mom said when she was alone upstairs, she would hear a man moaning. The sound followed her through all the bedrooms. It frightened her so bad she wouldn't go upstairs unless someone else was in the house.

Then one day, after dad had gone to work and we had left for school, mom said she went out the front door to visit a neighbor. When she returned, she heard music coming from inside the house, and the door had been locked from the inside! The police were called. One officer entered through an unlocked window, but they found no one inside, and no source for the music.

We moved after six months, and were happy to be leaving such a scary place. The neighbors said we had stayed longer than anyone else. The last I heard, the house was sitting empty. That doesn't surprise me.

The Man Who Was Buried Standing Up

If you happen to be driving south on Highway 11 a half dozen or so miles from downtown Roanoke, and the sun is just right, you might catch a glimpse of a crumbling, marbleized tomb that has stood as a solemn sentinel on the side of a sloping hill back-dropped by mountains for nearly two hundred years. Therein lies one of the most colorful legends of southwest Virginia.

Obscured today by dense underbrush, wild rosebushes and the roots, trunks and heavy limbs of centuries-old trees, the ten-foot-high tomb itself, and the wall that once surrounded it, lie in scattered ruins. The steep path to the craggy site high above Fotheringay Mansion has been long lost in jungle-like growth. Nevertheless, the tales persist, undiminished by the memory erosions of time. At this particular spot, on the hillside, many old-timers in the area will tell you that a man was buried here *standing up*.

His name was Colonel George Hancock, a spirited, charismatic and slightly eccentric gentleman who served as a Virginia congressman during George Washington's administration. He fought through the Revolutionary War, and it is said that his commander, General Pulaski, died in his arms at the siege of Savannah.

After the war, he settled in the tiny town of Elliston and, in 1796, bought Fotheringay and almost six hundred acres soon after that. According to the Virginia Landmarks Register, the great house was built soon afterward. It is, notes the register, "sited dramatically against the Blue Ridge Mountains overlooking the bottom lands of the south fork of the Roanoke River."

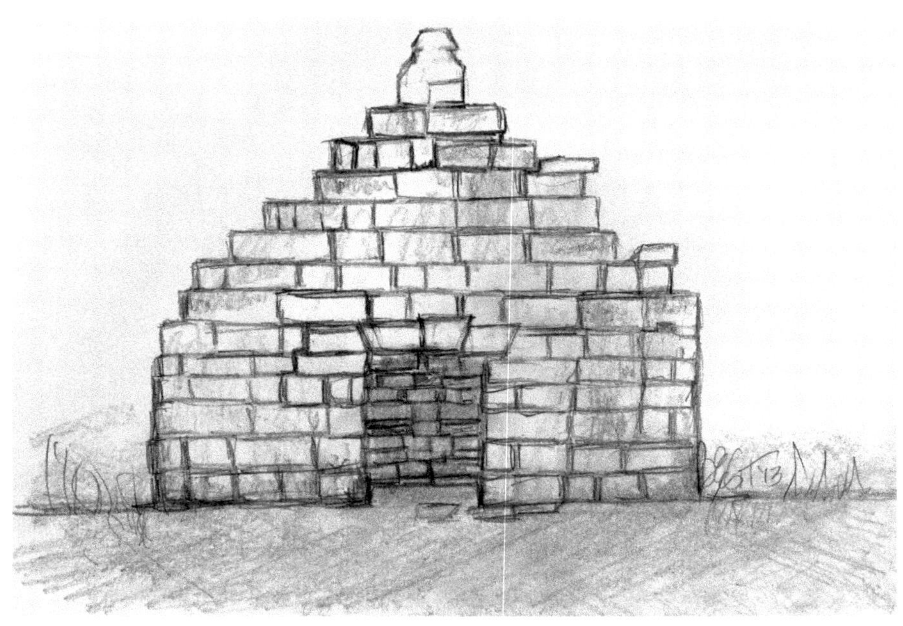

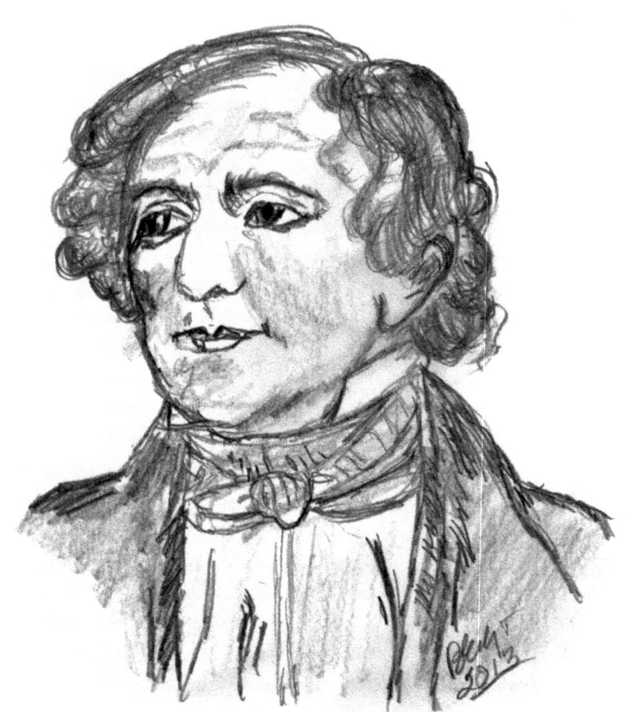

Above: Fotheringay, a veritable castle on the outskirts of Roanoke, was the home of Colonel George Hancock, who some believe was buried in his tomb (seen here) on the grounds standing up. *Illustration by Brenda E. Goens.*

Left: Colonel George Hancock. *Illustration by Brenda E. Goens.*

Hancock completed the central section and one wing. A second wing was added 150 years later. Oddly, Fotheringay was named for the English castle in which Mary, Queen of Scots, was beheaded.

This much is fact, but from here, the authenticity of the legend skates on thinner ice. It is known that in 1807, Hancock's daughter, Julia, married William Clark—of Lewis and Clark exploration fame and brother of George Rogers Clark. It is also widely held that Hancock had a strong distrust of the loyalty and willingness to work of his slaves. It is said that when he was running the estate himself, he kept it in pristine shape, but when military and political tenures kept him away from home, he would return to find it run-down and in disarray. This perhaps contributed to one of the colonel's zany characteristics, described by one writer thusly: "He was a gentleman of no uncertain temperament."

Julia died unexpectedly in 1820, and Colonel Hancock, grieving over her death, also passed away that year. One historian said that a double funeral service was held at the estate for father and daughter. However, the accounts of Hancock's burial vary considerably, depending on whom you read or ask. Many regional residents swear that the colonel was buried, at his specific request, standing up. It has been written that "to the rear of the old house and several hundred yards higher, is the tomb of Colonel Hancock, who was placed in it in an upright position so that he could always keep on eye on the slaves at work in the fields below, and keep them from loafing on the job."

Robert and Sarah Nutt, who inherited Fotheringay in the late 1950s, disagree with such a theory. Nutt reported that the bones in the vault were "mostly in niches" the last time he looked. An earlier owner, Eskridge Edmundson, recalled entering the vault as a young boy with several other men and "seeing the remains of skeletons on the sides on shelf like niches," with Hancock's bones in the middle, supposedly recognizable by the size of his skull. The other remains are those of Julia, son John and the colonel's mother-in-law.

It is, however, believed that the tall vault has been opened, or invaded, a number of times over the past two centuries. Mrs. Nutt, for example, said that curious Civil War soldiers "poked a hole in the roof and rummaged around a bit." One person who was steadfastly convinced that Hancock was buried in a standing position was C.C. Gasham. He was the Nutt's gardener and lived near the house all his life. As a youngster, he used to play at the tomb site. In 1979, at age sixty-seven, he told a reporter, "Folks have been in that vault and could have changed things." Others who deeply believed that the colonel was still standing in death and watching over them were Hancock's slaves. It is said that they toiled harder in the fields after he died than before his death.

And so, the legend endures. The colonel would have loved it.

The Man Who Was Buried Three Times

In the classic television series of a few years ago, *Lonesome Dove*, one of the most dramatic sequence of scenes involved Captain Call (Tommy Lee Jones) transporting the body of his lifelong friend, Gus (Robert Duvall), across the country from California to Texas, where Gus had said he wanted to be buried. It was a journey in the 1800s that took months to complete.

There is a real-life saga that tops it. It involved Major Charles Peter Deyerle, who was born just outside Salem, Virginia, in 1820. He was in the first graduating class of the Virginia Military Institute, joined the U.S. Army, served as a surgeon in the Mexican-American War under General Winfield Scott and later was posted in California. He died there unexpectedly in 1853 of gastritis and was buried.

When his family back in Salem heard the news of his death, they wanted his remains brought back to Virginia for interment in the family graveyard. And so, the major's brother, James, set out on what became an epic trip. He traveled by horseback, stagecoach, rail and riverboat from Salem to Washington, D.C., and got the necessary military permission to exhume and transfer the body. Then he went to New York and arranged passage on a steamboat.

It was well before the opening of the Panama Canal, so he had to go by foot and mule back across the Isthmus of Panama. He then went by rowboat three miles out to catch another ship on the Pacific Ocean side. When he finally reached California and had the coffin dug up, he ran into complications trying to get it aboard the ship for the return voyage. The ship's captain believed that the coffin signaled trouble and demanded that it be thrown overboard into the sea. But James and some other passengers finally convinced him to relent.

They started back. James was accompanied by a newspaper reporter named David Carter, who wrote about the venture. There were more problems when they reached the Panamanian Isthmus again. No one had ever carried a corpse across it, and none of the transportation agencies would touch it. James finally had to hire two local men and some mules for the arduous trek across Panama. Eventually, they sailed to New Orleans by way of Havana, Cuba, then up the Mississippi River and via land to Washington and finally down to Salem.

A funeral service was held at the family home. Reporter Carter wrote an epitaph: "He died far from home, traveling across two oceans. We bring his body to rest in its native vale. Here he was born, it is fit that here he should repose."

Ironically, though, this was not the end of Major Deyerle's travels. In 1902, the graves of the family were spaded up and removed to East Hill Cemetery in Salem, where they lie today, in center circle.

THE GHOST BUSTER OF ROANOKE

The late John Reiley was known for more than fifty years as the "Ghost Buster of Roanoke." His regional reputation as a "spirit detective," in fact, was so widespread that he got calls, letters and e-mails from people all across southwestern Virginia imploring him to come investigate and rid them of their resident ghosts. For decades, he traveled to every section of the city and to the hills and hollows bordering it to exorcise unwanted entities. And he did it with innovative and unusual methods, sometimes imitating or challenging the ghost to cause a reaction. Such creative means could well serve as lessons to today's plethora of amateur spirit hunters. Paranormal experts at Longwood College, Virginia Tech and the University of Virginia contacted him for consultation and advice on the supernatural. Reiley was happy to oblige and never charged a cent for his services. He loved doing it.

Over the years, Reiley collected hundreds of spectral legends across the commonwealth. He told, for instance, of a "haunted garden" along a fire trail on Catawba Mountain, where an eccentric millionaire and his wife once lived in a secluded home. There he found the remains of an ancient rock garden where the wife once spent most of her time. He said witnesses have reported that at the right time of the evening, they had seen the apparition of the millionaire's wife walking through the garden, talking to flowers that were no longer there.

When the historic Hotel Roanoke was closed for five years for renovations, Reiley said that staffers told him that one elevator would

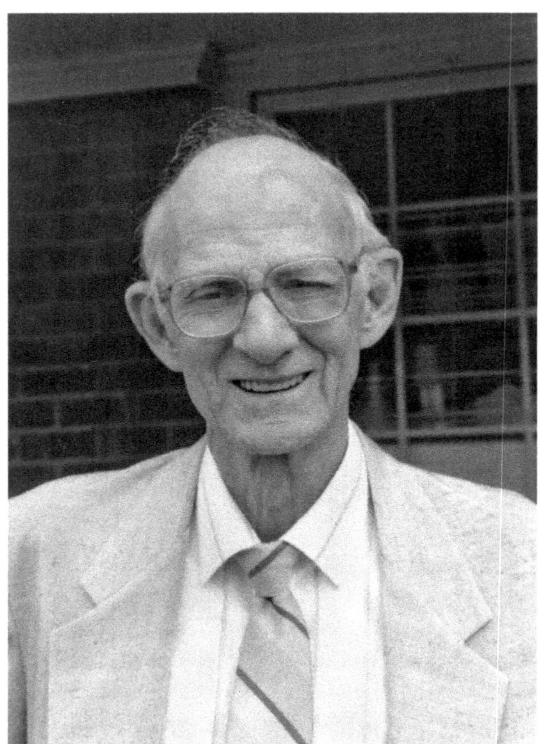

Left: The late John Reiley, known as the "Ghost Buster of Roanoke," investigated scores of ghostly legends in and around the city for more than half a century. *Photo by the author.*

Below: The Hotel Roanoke has been a favorite lodging, dining and entertainment center for decades. *Photo by Ruth Genter.*

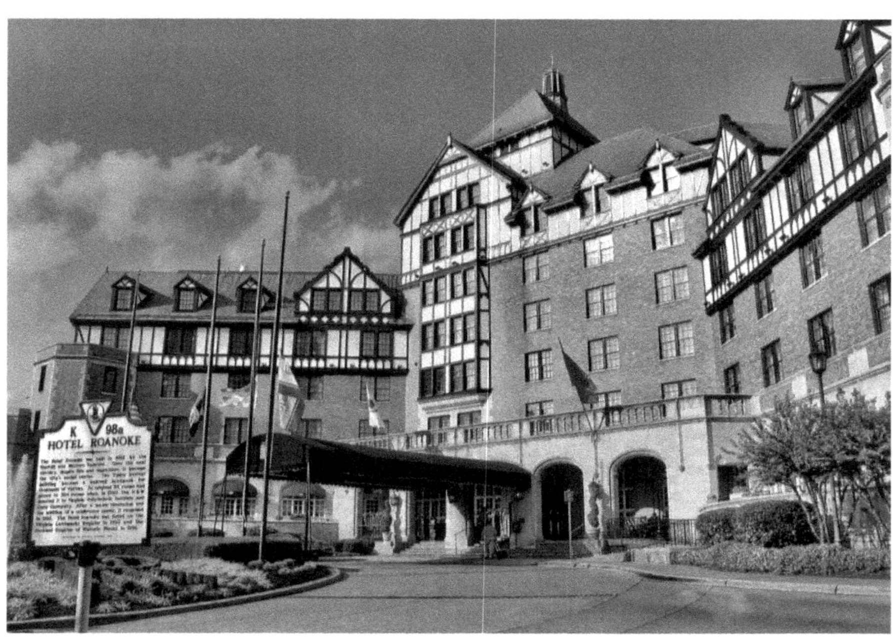

start on its own each morning and mysteriously rise to the fifth floor. A man in a neighboring county once invited Reiley to visit his home where, the man said, whenever he moved a chair in one room to the middle of the floor, the chair slid back on its own to its original position. Another time, a local man told Reiley to visit his stables. There was one stall there that no horse would enter. The legend was that a former owner once beat a horse to death in that stall.

Here is a sampling of some of the strange cases Reiley has personally experienced. In April 2000, he was called to a large house in the Roanoke suburbs by a woman named Ann Lucas. She said that the ghost of her late husband, a former vending machine executive, had returned to taunt her. She also said that she knew he had left a fortune of $350,000, but she couldn't find it.

> *She was a beautiful woman with long black hair. Her husband didn't treat her right. She called the ghost "Bam Bam" because it exhibited some poltergeist-like activities—you know, doors that slammed shut, lights that flickered on and off, that sort of thing. When I arrived, the lady said the house had ten rooms, and if I was any good, then I should be able to pick out which one her husband's ghost haunted. Well, I started out by putting a lighted candle in each room. A ghost will blow out a candle. I felt a cold spot in what was used as a lounge room. The candle was out. I said this is the room, and she said, "You're right." I knew I was right because when I entered the room a vase of flowers flipped over and two pictures on the wall crashed to the floor. One was a portrait of the lady.*

Reiley said that to bring out the spirit, he began bouncing up and down on a bed and hollering "Bam Bam" as loud as he could. He said that something he couldn't see steadied the bed and kept it from moving. Then, when he picked up the candle that had gone out, hot wax burned his hand. He examined it. Curiously, no wax had gathered on the side of the candle. "How could this have happened?" he asked.

"I cursed the ghost, and the lights started blinking," he said. "The more I fussed, the more they blinked. I recorded the whole thing on video tape." Reiley said that he never did uncover a clue as to where the money might be, but Mrs. Lucas did call him some time later and said that she hadn't heard from her dead husband anymore.

THE BELL THAT WOULDN'T RING

Cindy and Chip Harper of the nearby town of Buchanan called Reiley one day and asked him to come to their house and rid them of the ghost of a woman named Louise, whom they said was a nuisance. "She" would steal the baby's pacifier, turn lights on and off, start up appliances and things like that. When Reiley arrived, he found that Louise had been a teacher who had died in the house at about age eighty. He had an idea. Since Louise sometimes bothered the baby, he wrapped a doll in a blanket. He previously had tape recorded the voice of an infant crying. He played the tape over and over, and it apparently upset Louise, because the lights went on and off.

"I said if Louise is really still in this house, I'll find her," Reiley noted. He walked down a hallway and said that he entered a severe cold spot in front of the Harpers' son's room.

> *It was a hot day, and I walked right into that spot and then out of it. I figured this was where Louise hung out. Now, this is going to blow your mind. I asked for a bell. I thought since Louise had been a teacher, the bell would draw her out. So I walked down the hall toward that spot, ringing the bell as loud as I could.*
>
> *Now this is where it really gets good. When I got to that cold spot, no sound came out of the bell! There was not even a tinkle, although I was shaking the bell as hard as I could. Then something grabbed my arm. It wouldn't let me ring the bell. It got real cold. I thought I was having a heart attack! I got frightened. She had a strong hold, and when I finally got loose, even though it was icy cold, I was sweating.*

Just as suddenly as the bell was silenced and Reiley's arm was held, the grip loosened and the bell began ringing again. The cold spot evaporated. "I told the Harpers that Louise had been here, but she is gone now," Reiley said. "They called me later and told me they hadn't experienced her presence since. You see, ghosts are caught between two worlds. I try to find out the reason they are still here, and if you address that you can send them on. With Louise having been a teacher, for example, the bell was like a school bell and that's what drew her out."

THE LONELINESS OF JULIA

Several years ago, Reiley got a call from a woman in nearby Franklin County. She said that there was a ghost of a woman who lived in her house a long time ago. Reiley learned that the name of the spirit was Julia. She had lived in the house her entire life and had died when she was about eighty. As some point in her youth, Julia had fallen in love with a man of the sea. They were to be engaged, but after he left for a voyage, he never returned. Julia pined for him the rest of her life and apparently did after her death. Her ghost, the lady said, was still waiting for her lover's return.

The manifestations were many. Julia's apparition often descended the stairs in the late afternoon or early evening. Residents of the house both heard the footsteps and saw the figure. As her soft footsteps were heard, so, too, was the heavy tromping of booted feet coming up the walk outside the house. Julia would then seat herself at the dining room table, set with fancy cups and saucers. The trod outside was heard coming up the porch steps and approaching the front door. Then the sounds diminished, as if the "visitor" had disappeared. At this point, the image of Julia dematerialized.

Reiley checked out the house and found that a number of mirrors inside were broken. He attributed this to the fact that Julia was in the house by herself for a long time, and if she saw a fragment of a person (herself) in broken pieces, she wouldn't feel alone. To reach this particular spirit, Reiley came up with an ingenious scheme. He decided to dress himself in a style and manner reminiscent of the 1880s, supposedly when Julia's love affair took place. "I was going to dress up in an old sailor's uniform and sing old sea songs, like 'Blow the Man Down,'" Reiley recalled. "If the apparition saw and heard me, she might assume I was her missing lover, and this would complete her reason for staying here, and she could move on."

Alas, however, Reiley never got the chance to try his theory out. At the last minute, the woman who had called him told him not to do it. Her husband and children had grown to like Julia's ghost and were afraid that he would drive the spirit away.

THE "WHITE LADY" OF AVENEL

One of Virginia's most famous ghost legends is about the "White Lady" of Avenel, a historic house in the town of Bedford. Avenel was built in 1836, and like so many others in the commonwealth, the name comes from a novel written by Sir Walter Scott (such as Ivanhoe). In Scott's book *The Monastery*, he describes a most lively spirit, the White Lady of Avenel, who materializes at the site of a once majestic castle in Scotland. The White Lady's alleged first appearance in America is said to have occurred at the Bedford home in 1906 and was witnessed by, among others, Peggy Ballard Maupin, who lived in the house for more than eighty years.

"When we first saw her," Mrs. Maupin once said, "my mother and a whole crowd of us were at the end of the porch. It was about dusk when the White Lady walked up the lane that passed in front of the house. My mother said, 'Do you see what I see,' and just then the apparition disappeared in an old oak tree." Mrs. Maupin added that she and several others witnessed the figure, but no one could explain it. The vision was described as being a very fashionably dressed woman, but in clothes of an earlier era. She was carrying a white parasol. Mrs. Maupin believed that the figure might have been that of Frannie Steptoe Burwell, who lived in the house generations ago.

John Reiley had another theory as to the origin of the spirit. He thought that it may well have been the original ghost that Sir Walter Scott wrote about in the early 1800s. "Scott wrote about a castle that actually existed in Scotland," Reiley said. "And it was believed that when the house in Bedford was built, some of the bricks from that castle were imported. Could not the spirit of the White Lady have come with them?"

Armed with this novel idea, Reiley was invited one day several years ago to visit Avenel in Bedford in the hopes of resurrecting the ghost of the White Lady. He decided that his best chance of raising the spirit would be to read chants used in Scott's book. So he went to the majestic tree (which he said was a magnolia tree, not an oak), the spot where the White Lady had vanished in the 1906 sighting.

Reiley said that just as he finished the chant lines, he felt a strange sensation, as if an unseen presence was there. He looked up. Shocked, he saw a huge magnolia pod from high in the tree falling straight at his head. He dodged, and the pod hit his foot. "Was that a sign from another world, or what?" he exclaimed. He took the pod home with him to Roanoke and put it in his freezer. He showed it to anyone who asked.

Three years later, Reiley went back to Avenel in Bedford to attend the wedding reception of a friend of his at the house. In the dark that evening, he went out to the same magnolia tree, picked up another pod and hid it. Later, as he was leaving, he went to retrieve the pod, but it had vanished.

A Most Fearful Encounter

John Reiley was not afraid of ghosts. In fact, he found them most fascinating creatures. He would go anywhere, on a moment's notice, in search of a spirit. But there was one time, in 1996, when he was terribly shaken by a harrowing experience at an old barn. He had been invited by the owner of a farm to visit what had been described as a "haunted barn." He had not been told anything about the past history of the place. So, armed with his camcorder, he drove over to the abandoned plantation.

As he approached the barn, he said, "The back of my hair started coming up. I could feel a pressure I had never felt before. When I opened the door to the barn, an overwhelming odor nearly knocked me out." When he passed through the dark doorway, he later told *Roanoke Times* staff writer Mike Allen, "I was so completely smothered, like something was trying to get inside of me, to take over my body. I could feel sort of moans and cries of pain. It was like some kind of unseen force was trying to take over me." Reiley added that he had never been so scared in his life. "I had to think hard of pleasant things to get out of the grip of this evil spirit," he said.

He didn't wait around. He got out of the barn as fast as he could. Later, he contacted the owner and learned that when the plantation had been an active farm, in pre–Civil War days, the overseer had been cruel to the slaves there. He had beaten several slaves to death in the barn. When the owner found out about this, he was so incensed that he killed the overseer. "That is what I felt when I entered that barn," Reiley said. "To this day, the restless spirits of the slaves still linger there. I won't go back there. No sir!"

Some Mysteries Endure

There are some cases that Reiley said may be unsolvable. "Let me tell you one that will knock your socks off," he once said. "There is an old church, Mount Olive Church, in Ivanhoe, near Fort Chiswell, where in 1938 a woman was to get married there. The groom to be had just said his vows, and as the bride to be was about to say hers, the church doors suddenly sprang open, the wind blew out all the candles and the lights went out. It got dark quick. It took about five minutes to get the lights on again, and when they came on, the bride had vanished and was never seen again!"

The Gold Earring

John Reiley was once given a photo of an old house on Maple Avenue in Roanoke, between Third Street and Franklin Avenue. It was taken by a local doctor. There supposedly was no one in the house at the time, but as the picture was being snapped, there appeared to be someone or something peering out an attic window. The doctor told Reiley that he then searched the house to see who it was, but there was no one there.

Reiley had the photo blown up and examined it carefully. "I believe it is the spirit of a large black woman, probably a nanny, who may have been a servant in the house long ago," he said. "She is wearing a white turban and one gold earring. Now, I have done some research, and I found that it was common for such servants, and even slaves of an earlier time, to wear two gold earrings if they were married. However, if they were widowed or divorced, they were allowed to wear only one earring. The only other thing I can tell you about this picture is that there is a very sad expression on her face. I could tell this by looking through a powerful magnifying glass."

Dispelling a Dark Rumor

In 2001, Tricia and Kelly Scott bought a century-old house on Oakland Boulevard in the northwest section of Roanoke on land formerly known as the Nininger estate. There had been some dark rumors about the house, and Tricia wanted to find out about them, so she called John Reiley and asked him to come over and look into it. The rumor Tricia had heard from old neighborhood gossip was that a woman had been murdered in the house and her body buried in the dirt cellar. Allegedly, years later, a child digging in the dirt came upon the skeletal remains of the woman. Tricia was concerned because she said her husband often worked late at night, and she would be alone in the house with her two-year-old daughter. She didn't want a sad or perhaps evil spirit confronting her. Could Reiley find out if such a ghost existed?

He took one small candle and descended the steep, narrow stairway into the dank cellar. There was a dirt floor and dirt walls. "I wondered why no one ever had the basement finished," Reiley mused. He then methodically stepped, foot by foot, around the perimeter of the cellar. Thirty minutes later, he came back up the stairs with a smile on his face.

"Well," he told Tricia and Kelly, "I can tell you for certain that no one was ever murdered and buried down there. There is no human spirit of any kind." Reiley explained his methodology. If the candle he carried was blown out and there was no wind, it would be indicative of the presence of a spirit. Another sign would be a frosty cold spot. Reiley found neither.

"Now I will tell you something about that basement," he said. "They used to keep horses down there." How did he know this? "I found some traces of hay, and there are places cut out in the dirt walls that are remindful of old stables," Reiley answered. "Also, there is an entrance where the horses could be led straight into the basement. So if there are any spirits at all, they might be of horses. I bet if you played a tape of a horse neighing, you'd hear some loud stomping of hooves down there."

Tricia smiled. Her mind had been put at ease.

A Phantom Dog and Rattling Chains

The following is John Reiley's account of a haunting he investigated in an old farm on the outskirts of Roanoke.

> *Granny Harris Karns told her granddaughter, Doris Toms, about a ghost dog that haunted a fancy farmhouse in the nineteenth century. Robert Kelso first owned the farm and house. His wife died, leaving only his dog, Tramp. Kelso had been scared that Tramp might leave him, so he put him on a chain that was connected to a block. The chain extended just outside the front door. At night, Tramp would howl and try to get away from the chain, then he died still attached to the chain and block.*
>
> *A few years later, Kelso passed on, leaving the farm to his only living relative, Susan Hooper. Susan needed a sharecropper to run the farm. John and Hattie Karns agreed to share the work, provided they could live in the basement of the farmhouse. Mrs. Hooper agreed.*
>
> *Hattie said she and John Karns spent many nights awakened by the low moan of a dog, the rattling of chains and the slipping of a heavy block. They checked the basement and upstairs, but they never found even a sign of a dog, chains or a block. Like I have often said, some mysteries are never solved.*

If there ever was a way to unlock such inexplicable paranormal events, John Reiley, the Ghost Buster of Roanoke, was the man to call.

The Paranormal Paintings of Eddie Maxwell

Self-made artist Eddie Maxwell of Roanoke died in September 2009, but like the works of the old masters, his bizarre paranormal paintings live on. To those who are fascinated by the supernatural, they are highly prized. You see, Maxwell and others claimed that things came to life in his art, literally. The late John Reiley of Roanoke, who studied psychic phenomena for more than fifty years, once said, "If you watch his paintings closely, things *move* in them! What would you say if you saw birds flying right at you from the canvas? And the birds weren't there when you first looked? Maxwell has a couple in one picture, and if you look closely and hard enough, the couple starts dancing right in front of you! In another one, a woman with wings seems to appear out of nowhere." He continued, "I've seen this, and I know people will think I'm crazy, but it's true. He says he paints as if he's possessed by some presence. I tell you it's the most extraordinary thing I've ever seen!"

Another curious note to add is the fact that Maxwell, like Grandma Moses, didn't begin painting until late in life. He was sixty when he started. There was no indication of his unusual talent in his background. He grew up in Bluefield, West Virginia, and after service in the U.S. Army, he spent eighteen years working for the Norfolk and Western Railroad. Following this, he went to a beauty school and opened a hair salon in Arlington. It was a success, and before long, he owned four such shops and had forty employees.

After a quarter of a century, the intense pressure of running such a business took its toll. In 1989, Maxwell suffered a seizure. It was serious. Doctors didn't know if he would live through it or not, and even if he did,

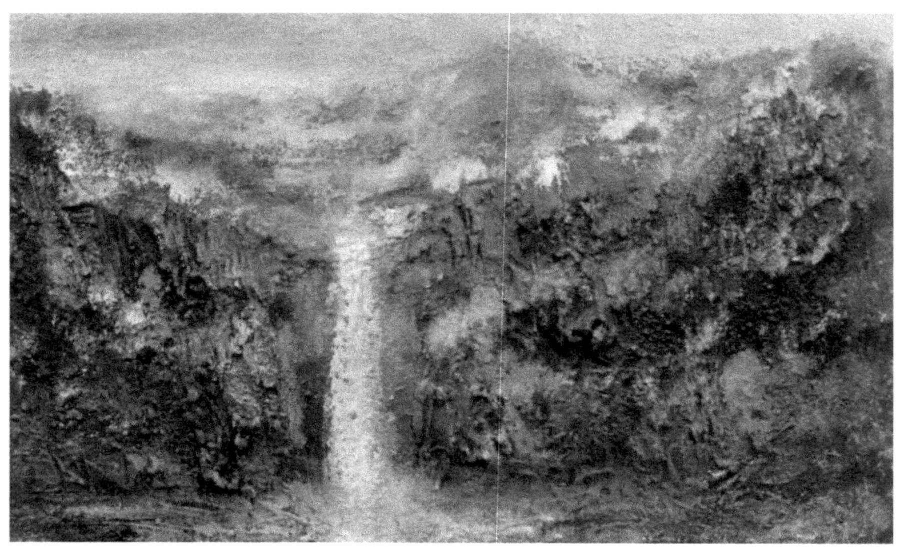

The paintings from the late Roanoke artist Eddie Maxwell were believed to have been enhanced by paranormal entities. *Photo by the author.*

they were not sure that he would still be able to function as an active person. "Stress nearly killed me," he said. He sank into a deep state of depression.

Then coincidence—or providence or whatever you want to call it—occurred. He found an old discarded canvas and started to paint. He had no particular subject in mind, and he seemed to be working with intensity, drive and direction he had never before experienced. When he finished, he had painted an inspiring portrait of Jesus Christ on the cross. And it appeared to have been done with a flair and skill far beyond anything he had ever achieved before.

"I really didn't know how it happened," he said in retrospect. "It was almost as if some presence, or something, was guiding my hand as I worked." Maxwell took this as a sign of divine intervention. And so he began to paint. Sometimes he would be moved by what he believed was a spiritual presence that compelled him to work. He would get up in the middle of the night and at times not even realize what he was creating. The next day, when he viewed the canvas, he would be amazed at what he saw.

Eventually, this unseen "presence" came to be known to him as "Moneneer."

> *It was like he was assigned to me. He was my inspiration. Whenever things weren't going well, or I was feeling depressed, Moneneer would communicate with me. He would talk to me. He would get me through my*

down times and encourage me to continue my work. If I didn't snap right out of being depressed, he would scold me, and tell me to have faith.

At first, all this scared me. I didn't understand it. Then, one day, a minister friend of mine came over, and he told me not to be afraid. He said when Moneneer talks to me, just to listen and to take things in stride. He said it was like an omen that was telling me my mission in life was to paint and to just go with it, not question it.

As his art progressed—he painted mostly landscapes in oil—he began to notice something very strange. After he had completed a painting and set it up to dry, he would, a day or two later, notice some "additions" to his work. "I can't explain it, I don't know how it happens, but people started showing up in the paintings—people I didn't put there!" he said.

For example, he once painted a café scene reminiscent of the work of a French impressionist. There were chairs and tables on several levels of flooring. He added about five people, sitting at one of the tables. In time, according to Maxwell, John Reiley and other witnesses, the other tables in the picture began filling up on their own with people. Today, there are more than fifty men and women seated at the café. Maxwell swears that he didn't put them there—they somehow kind of showed up on their own.

In another rendering, of an outdoor wedding scene, Maxwell included just the bride and groom and a few others. Today, there are more than forty people on the grounds. There is a couple standing in the middle of the picture. Several witnesses contend that if you concentrate attention on the couple, you will see them move forward and dance before your eyes. Maxwell said that he once brought home a woman to view his work. She looked carefully at one painting and told him that she didn't know he had painted Elvis in it. He didn't know it either. But when he looked—sure enough, there was Elvis.

John Reiley said that for one painting, if you look hard enough at a woman in it, she develops wings. In another, a man is said to "turn" and look at a woman seated next to him. "In Maxwell's *Christ on a Cross*," Reiley added, "at first it appears to be just splotches in the background, but after a while, these splotches turn into people at the feet of Christ." Reiley believes that Maxwell was visited by a "force" that transmitted energy to him.

At first, when Maxwell saw the "extra" people and other things in his paintings, he thought they were out of place and he erased them. But then he learned that, while he couldn't explain the phenomena, maybe they should be left there.

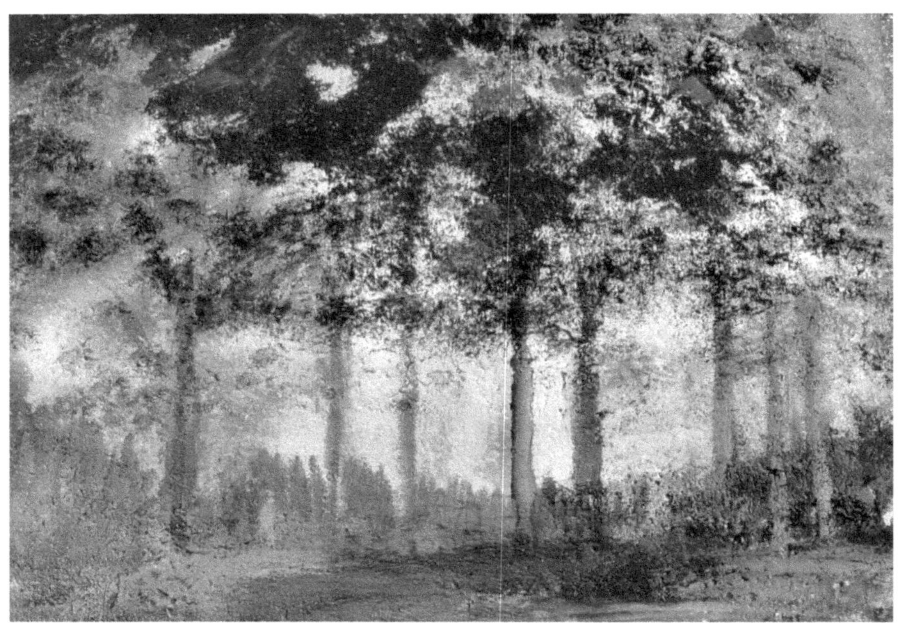

Paintings by Roanoke artist Eddie Maxwell. *Photos by Brenda E. Goens.*

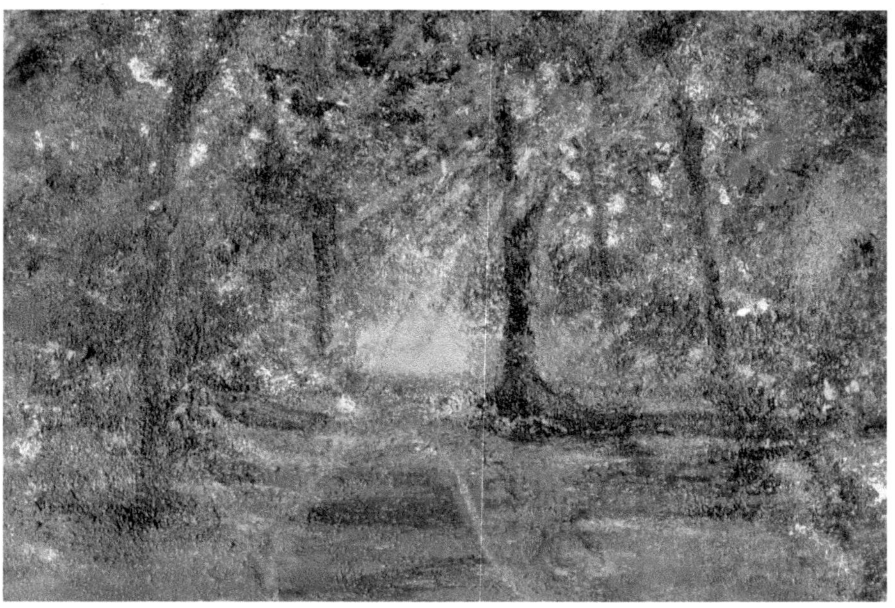

It can be said without question that his paintings are unique, and Maxwell was well into his seventies before his work was discovered and appreciated. At an exhibit in 2007, several paintings were sold, at prices ranging into the thousands. Some of his work is remindful of the late nineteenth- and early twentieth-century output of French impressionism. There are scenes of an almost eerie quality of trees, mountains, parks and waterfalls. Maxwell's celestial use of sunlight rays and reflections has been praised by art critics as being unusually effective.

How do the figures mysteriously appear in his paintings? Do they materialize in a supernatural manner, or is there a more rational explanation? There is perhaps a clue in a publicity sheet printed about Maxwell: "When a painting is completed, the artist steps back to review his work. He is astonished in what appears there because he never consciously put it there." Jonathan McGraw, owner of a Roanoke art gallery that exhibited some of Maxwell's paintings, said that visitors saw some of the "added images" and didn't see others. McGraw himself believes in the visions and added, "I trust that everything he experienced was real to him. I have no reason to doubt that he was telling the truth."

I met with Maxwell in Roanoke in 2001, first at the Vantage Center, where his work was being shown and later at his studio. I saw the paintings. I didn't see anything move. At one point, Maxwell unveiled his latest canvas. It was a striking scene of a cascading waterfall. He showed me a white dove that appeared about one-third of the way across the painting from the left, winging to the right. "Yesterday, that dove was over here," he said, pointing six inches further left on the canvas.

I can't tell you if Maxwell unconsciously paints in the "extras" in his work or if he does it somehow in an altered state, as has been suggested. Or do the figures just inexplicably show up on their own? I don't pretend to have the answer. But I was impressed. I bought two of his paintings. If something suddenly appears that wasn't there before, I'll know.

Stark Fear Strikes the City

Following are two terrifying incidents in the history of Roanoke. While neither directly relates to ghostly activity, there are some strange paranormal overtones.

The Riot of 1893

On September 21, 1893, Mrs. Sallie Bishop of Botetourt County came to Roanoke to sell her fruit and vegetables at the city farmers' market. She was approached by an African American named Thomas Smith. He said that Mrs. Hicks, who lived nearby, wanted sixty cents' worth of wild grapes for preserving if Mrs. Bishop would deliver them to her house. He told her that he would show her the way. She followed him several blocks, through an alleyway and into a building. There, he slammed the door shut and demanded her money. Horrified, Mrs. Bishop gave him her pocketbook. She had two dollars in it. Then she pleaded for her life. Smith, however, drew a razor and attacked her. She managed to knock the razor away, but he beat her with a bat and choked her senseless. Leaving her for dead, he ran toward Woodland Park.

About half an hour later, Mrs. Bishop regained consciousness and, caked in her own blood, staggered her way out of the building and reached help. As she was telling what had happened, two men several blocks away saw Smith running away and decided to chase him. Ironically, one of the men was W.P. Blount, Mrs. Bishop's cousin. As they did, others rode up on horseback to

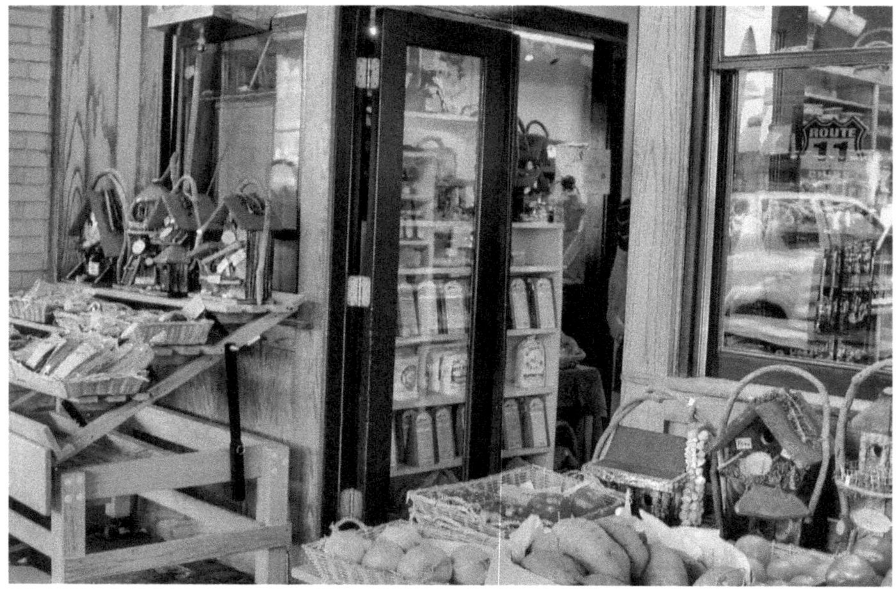

Everything from fresh fruits and vegetables to fine arts and collectables are daily on display at the historic marketplace in downtown Roanoke. *Photo by Ruth Genter.*

tell of Smith's assault. They caught him minutes later near the old Wood Novelty Works.

A detective brought Smith back to town and took him to a saloon where Mrs. Bishop was having her wounds attended to. Though she could hardly see, as she had lost the sight of one eye in the struggle, she identified him as her assailant by his hat. By then, a crowd of enraged citizens had gathered, yelling for blood. The detective dodged the crowd by telling them that Mrs. Bishop had not identified Smith. He then sped him on horseback to the city jail.

When the mob, now estimated at about 1,500 people, learned the truth, they went to the jail and demanded Smith's release to them. The Roanoke Light Infantry and the Jeff Davis Rifles of nearby Salem were alerted to stand by. Soldiers marched to the front of the jail and stood guard. By this time, word had reached Mrs. Bishop's friends and neighbors in Botetourt, and they headed straight for Roanoke.

At 8:00 p.m., the angry mob made a mad rush at the front of the jail, but the attack was repulsed when soldiers drew their bayonets. A few minutes later, hundreds of men forced their way into the west side of the building and stormed toward Smith's cell. Suddenly, a shot rang out, then another. Next, all hell broke loose. It was later estimated that more than 150 pistol and rifle shots had been fired, although it was never learned who had shot first. In the aftermath, nine prominent citizens were dead and dozens of others wounded, some critically. In the furious crossfire, hundreds of others hastily retreated to safety.

A short time later, the mob reassembled. The people marched to the mayor's house to demand Smith's release to them. When the mayor was found not to be home, they searched the town. The vigilantes then raided some hardware stores and commandeered rifles, pistols and cartridges. Judge John Woods and J. Allen Watts, leading citizens, attempted to reason with the crowd, but they were shouted down. As this was happening, Smith was spirited from the jail by two police officers and taken through an alley to the banks of the Roanoke River in a desperate attempt to elude the pursuers.

The mob then charged the jail a third time, only to find no prisoner behind bars. The men then fanned out throughout the area in a determined search for Smith. At about 3:00 a.m., the officers who had taken Smith thought things had quieted down enough to bring him back to the jail. On the way, however, they were ambushed by about fifteen men hiding in a vacant lot and armed with guns. The police were forced to surrender the prisoner. The men then dragged Smith to a hickory tree, put a noose around his neck and hanged him.

He was left overnight dangling there, and during the next day, thousands came to view the corpse. Then these morbid spectators stripped Smith of his clothes and fought for "souvenir" pieces of the rope. The crowds stayed in the street surrounding the tree all night long. Then someone got the idea to yank the body down, haul it to the mayor's house and bury it in his front yard. They were upset at the mayor because they mistakenly believed that he had ordered the first shot at the jail. Reverend W.C. Campbell, however, talked them out of this impromptu burial, but that did not satisfy the sadistic bent of the crowd. They next carried the corpse to the edge of the river and placed it atop a pile of firewood. They soaked everything in coal oil and then lit it, cremating the body. This grisly ritual drew hundreds more.

To help restore order, 150 reputable citizens were sworn in as special deputies, but they were not needed. The number of those dead and wounded, and the atrocious attitude of the mob before, during and after the lynching, had shocked and sobered the city. Several men were indicted for the shootings at the jail, and a few were sentenced to prison.

There was, as Roanoke author Raymond Barnes noted in his book on the history of the city, a curious footnote to the tragedy. The tree from which Smith was hanged died soon after. As Barnes noted, "Immediately, the superstitious credited the lynching and the foul deed as arousing the fury of providence to destroy the instrument of vengeance."

THE DAY EVERYONE FLED TOWN

On July 4, 1901, a second, most extraordinary event occurred in Roanoke. It began a month earlier when an itinerant African American preacher came to town. He was described as being tall and angular and having unusually long eyelashes, presenting a most formidable appearance. He called himself a prophet, and apparently, many believed him, for when he preached great crowds gathered.

He said he received "warnings" of impending tragedies from "an inner voice." To back this up, he told his followers that he had predicted the great Johnstown flood, and all those who had heeded his advance advice had been saved from drowning. He then delivered a bombshell. He said that his inner voice urged him to tell the people of Roanoke that their city would be destroyed by fire at 4:00 p.m. on July 4, 1901, and that "by a living flame all who remained here would perish miserably."

Then a strange thing happened: people believed him. Word of the coming calamity spread through the town among both blacks and whites. To enhance the fears of the superstitious, a terrible heat wave hit Roanoke, and a man dropped dead on a city street from heat prostration on July 2. By the next day, people began leaving the town, taking bundles of food and clothing with them. One man said that he was heading for the hills, and when asked why, according to author Raymond Barnes, he replied, "Ain't you hear dat Sodom and Gomorrah is on the way to Roanoke? Yessir, that town is going up in fire!"

On the morning of the Fourth of July, it was reported that the roads leading out of the city were clogged with heavy outbound traffic. Many rented rigs and transfer wagons and packed up their entire families to escape. Barnes said that many white citizens crammed Vinton-Salem streetcars—not out of fear of the predicted holocaust, they said, but "just in case."

At about 4:00 p.m., the hour of doom that had been predicted, thunderous skies opened up and a deluge drenched Roanoke. The so-called prophet's inner voice had failed, and there were a lot of embarrassed people who then timidly reentered the town. The itinerant preacher, meanwhile, had moved on to Boone's Mill and Rocky Mount to warn the citizens there of yet another pending disaster.

Diary of a Haunted House

Donna Dean fell in love with the house the first time she saw it. "When we rode up the mountain and rounded a bend and I first saw it, I said, 'This is the house I want.' It was love at first sight," she remembered. "I had fantasized about the house ever since I was a little girl even though I had never seen it before." It is a large Victorian, three stories tall, with huge white columns and a commanding view of the surrounding countryside. It is on Bent Mountain, eight miles from the center of Roanoke. Donna, a former weathercaster for a local television station, and her husband, Barney, bought the place in 1999. It had been built in 1908.

"I didn't know it at the time," Donna said, "but this had been my grandmother's dream house years ago." The first time Donna's mother saw it after the Deans had bought it, she said, "I don't believe it!" Then she told her daughter that when she was a little girl, her mother, Rosa, Donna's grandmother, and grandfather, Joseph, would take her across Bent Mountain after church on Sunday afternoon drives. They would pass the house, and Rosa always commented about how much she loved it. "What a striking coincidence," Donna said. "Can you imagine, we both fell in love with the same house two generations apart. It was like it was predestined for me to have this house." Donna named the house Rosemont after her grandmother, who died in 1977.

Donna and Barney did some research. They knew that Bent Mountain had long been famous for its rich apple orchards, and at one time, there had been more than eight hundred bearing trees on their property. The house

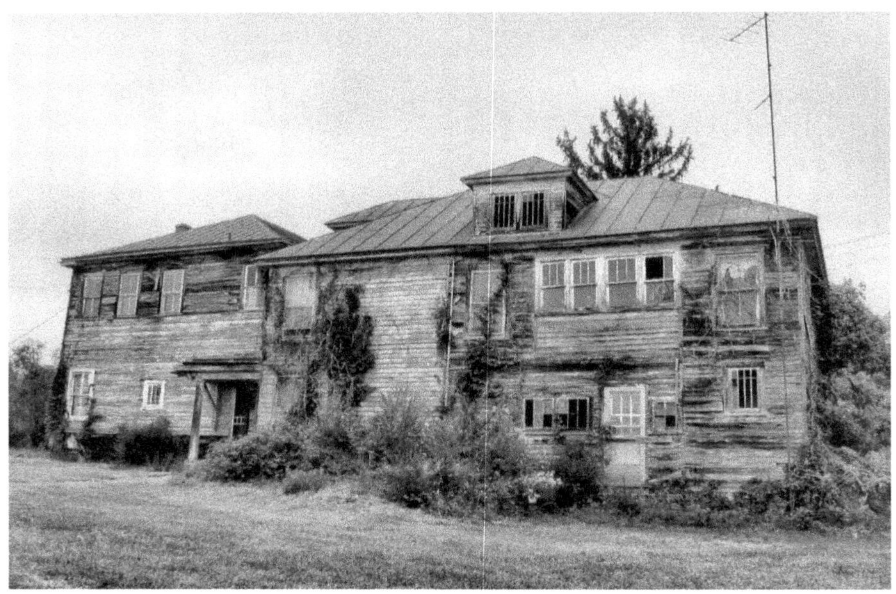

A haunted-looking house on the outskirts of Roanoke. *Photo by Ruth Genter.*

had been owned, early in the twentieth century, by Libbey Cameron Shockey, a prominent businessman in the Roanoke area. Shockey, all six-foot-five and three hundred pounds of him, had later become a coffin maker, with an eccentric bent. To advertise his wares, for example, he placed his coffins out in the yard so prospective customers could see them as they drove by.

Paranormal activity began almost from the moment the Deans moved in and started renovating Rosemont. Manifestations ran the gamut. There were unexplained footsteps; doors that slammed shut by themselves; loud, crashing noises with no apparent source; and faint glimpses of wispy substances out of the corner of the eye that disappeared only to mysteriously resurface in surprising locations.

"I felt like spirits were here," Donna recalled, "but they were not negative ones. They watch over and protect me." She added that she was "somehow drawn" to contact a woman she had never met before, Deborah Carvelli, a psychic from Roanoke. Debbie taught classes in parapsychology and on paranormal activities at Virginia Western Community College in the city. "I called her one day," Donna said, "and only a minute or so into the conversation, she informed me that there was a woman who was with me all the time in the house. She said her name was Rose, or Roselyn or something like that. I was astounded because I had not told her anything about my family."

Over the next several months, Donna and Debbie were to form a special bond, almost as if they had been sisters in a past life. Debbie would bring students from her classes to Rosemont without giving them any information on the house, Donna's family or the strange activity that was taking place there. The students sensed things the minute they entered the grounds. One, in fact, sat down and began drawing sketches of coffins. When asked why, she said that she didn't really know. It just happened.

When the author visited Rosemont in 2001 with Debbie and Jackie, Debbie's teenage daughter, Jackie said that she saw the image of a woman sitting by an attic window. When Jackie was shown a portrait of a woman inside the house, she immediately said that was the person she had seen—it was Donna's grandmother.

Donna began keeping journals of the inexplicable events that were taking place in the house. She made detailed entries, documenting each occurrence and the time it happened. It is a rare diary of the paranormal. Following are selected verbatim passages describing what she, her husband and others experienced over a specified period of time, beginning late in 1999.

> *November 29: After only three nights in our new home, I awoke around 7:30 a.m. and went into the guest bathroom so I wouldn't disturb Barney's sleep. I suddenly heard three loud knocks on one of the closed doors in the hallway. The sound reverberated throughout the upstairs. I assumed Barney had awakened and did that to scare me, but when I looked, no one was there and I found Barney still in bed asleep.*
>
> *First week of December: Our third week in the house. Barney was out of town. I was taking a bath, watching the water fill, when the hot water faucet turned off by itself. I was dumbfounded. Testing the faucet, I had to apply a lot of pressure to turn the water off myself. I then realized it was impossible for this to happen without someone pushing it, but it wasn't me!* [This occurred a number of times over the next few months.]
>
> *January 1, 2000: This was the only bizarre incident to upset me so far. Barney had arisen early to take the dogs outside. I was exhausted and in a deep sleep. I awoke to loud pounding on the window downstairs. It was Barney beating on the glass. He said he had been locked out, but this was impossible, because there was no lock on the front door! He said it was as though something was applying force from the other side of the door. I was very upset, and then said out loud, "Whoever did this, don't do it again!"*

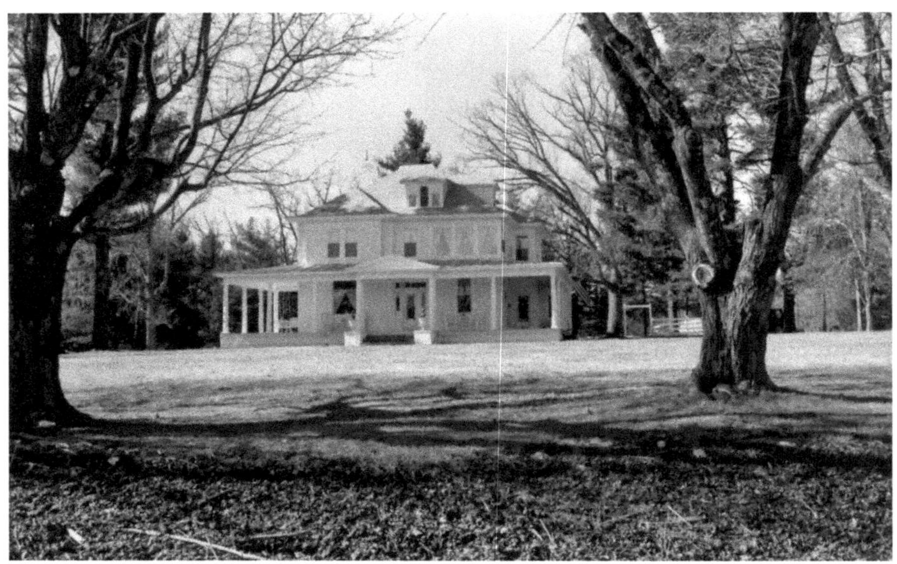

At Rosemount, on Bent Mountain, just outside of Roanoke, a diary was kept documenting scores of paranormal happenings at the home. *Photo by the author.*

January 2: We were watching a movie on TV downstairs. Suddenly, we heard a loud crash upstairs. Barney went up and told me my cement pedestal had fallen to the floor. This couldn't have happened unless it had been pushed, because I had carefully positioned it against the wall.

January 8: The brass bell in the den began swinging on its own. I'm beginning to think it may have a connection with my daughter, Kristen, who died, because every time I have noticed the bell swaying, I was thinking of her. I have a strong feeling that Kristen may be manipulating the bell in an attempt at communication. It always happens when I'm thinking of her or talking about her.

February 22: Deborah Carvelli brought her class to tour the house. Several students said they saw the figure of an old lady with dark hair in a bun, wearing a long dress, standing in front of the fireplace in the living room. They said she resembled the woman in a portrait on the fireplace mantel, the portrait of my great grandmother, Minnie Steele Sink! Others reported they saw the apparition of a young woman with long brown curly air and blue eyes, standing near the front door. I showed them a photo my oldest daughter, Kristen, now deceased, and they said the image strongly favored her.

February 28: I made several trips up and down the stairs. Each time I walked through the entrance parlor, I smelled a very powerful fragrance of roses. I had no fresh flowers in the house at the time. [This, too, occurred often.]

March 15: Our antique clock in the den gonged four times, then once more five minutes later, and again 20 minutes after that. This was odd because the gong mechanism wasn't wound up for it to function, and it hadn't gonged for several years!

April 6: I was outside walking around with the puppies. Something had been telling me for the last few days to look for something close to the house, although I didn't have any idea what it was. Near the kitchen window I saw a shiny object partially covered with dirt. I picked it up and brushed it off. It was a small silver cross engraved with the words, "God Loves You!" I felt an overwhelming sense of love. I knew instantly this was a gift from the spirits that reside in the house. They wanted me to have it.

June 30: A picture of Barney, in a wrought iron stand, flew across the downstairs hallway, and was witnessed by two workmen who were in the house.

August 23: This incident is one of the most profound I experienced. I was in the laundry room upstairs and had just come out and shut the door. I even heard the latch close. I took a few steps and all of a sudden the laundry door opened by itself. I walked over to the door and said, "Okay, if you are really there, close it!" And, without hesitation, the door closed by itself.

August 25: As I opened the bedroom door to go downstairs, heavy pipe smoke hit me in the face. Barney doesn't smoke a pipe. [This occurred several more times. All during this period, there were many other strange happenings, too numerous to include, such as light switches being turned on and off by unseen hands, electric appliances that switched on and off on their own, doors opening and closing by themselves, untouched objects moving and things missing only to turn up in surprising locations.]

October 9: This is extremely significant because it represents the first time I actually saw anything in the eleven months we had been in the house. Barney was in the kitchen, and I was lying on the couch in the den, watching TV. I glanced at the big window and saw a white blur flash across the room. I thought it was Barney, but he was still in the kitchen.

In her first year of residency, Donna recorded eighty-seven separate incidents that she felt were unexplainable by rational or logical means.

January 9, 2001: It was the coldest day of the year so far, and the furnace went out. I called Barney. When he came home he went into the basement to check. He came up and told me, "You're not going to believe this. It's the strangest thing." Something, he said, had pulled the plug that controls the furnace out of the socket in the wall. This plug can't be dislodged or loosely fall out by itself. It had to be physically pulled out of the wall. Neither of us had done it, and we were the only ones in the house. Coincidentally, we had been hearing a lot of curious noises in the basement during that time.

March 7: Tigger, our cat, seemed transfixed, staring at something I couldn't see in the den. His head was tilted back as if he was looking at something taller than him. He was mesmerized for some time.

April 12: Debbie Carvelli and another of her classes came by for a visit. She makes it a point not to tell any of the students anything about the house or the happenings here. She wants them to relate any feelings they have without having any previous knowledge. This time one girl, "Anita," seemed particularly sensitive. She told me she sensed my grandmother in the rose room upstairs, and she described her to me, not just physically, but her personality as well—and she was precisely accurate! She then said my grandmother's first name was Rose and her middle name had an E and two L's in it. I was astounded. Grandma's name was Rosa and her middle name was Ella! It is not a common name.

May 21: I had just finished my bath and was standing in front of the mirror in the upstairs guest room, when out of the corner of my eye, my peripheral vision picked up movement of a gray mist passing by me from the door on the left. This mist was approximately the size of a beach ball and floating four feet above the floor. When I turned around, it disappeared. This was only my second "sighting" in the house.

Later that night, as I walked into the bedroom, I was carrying our teacup poodle, Toby, in one hand and a drink in the other. I put Toby down to open the door, but when I reached back down for him he was gone. I searched everywhere, downstairs and up, but couldn't find him anywhere. Finally, when I pulled back the bed covers, there he was, underneath! Now, how did he get there? Our bed is four feet tall and there is no way a dog that tiny could have leaped up there. Barney had been asleep in the bed the whole time and never woke up. This is something I have never been able to explain.

July 26: The most amazingly unexplainable thing just happened. I was in the master bath preparing for bed. I always bring a glass of apple juice upstairs with me, and sometimes there is a half full glass on my wash basin the next morning because I didn't drink it all the night before. As I poured out the stale liquid, something fell out of the bottom of the glass. It looked like a small piece of ice, but on closer inspection I discovered it was the stone missing from the ring Barney had bought me. That stone had fallen out of the ring three months ago! I really had felt that it was gone. How could it suddenly appear in a glass of juice? It couldn't have fallen out in the ice bin because that container had been completely emptied many times since the stone was lost.

A special note: earlier that day I asked grandma and Kristen to give me a sign that they were still around. I believe this was their answer.

July 26: Debbie Carvelli and her students arrived again. During their visit one incident piqued my interest. One student, a school teacher, said she saw a woman in a long dark brown dress, with a high collar which she thought to be from around the early 1900s. She said the woman had dark hair pulled back in a bun and deep set eyes. She added that the woman didn't seen to notice the students in the room, appeared to be very demure, and walked past the group and vanished. The student then picked out a woman in a photograph that she said was identical to the apparitional woman she had seen. It was a picture of my great grandmother, Minnie Steele Sink, grandma Rosa's mother! She had been glimpsed in the yellow rose room where Rosa, too, has been seen many times by others.

In all, during this twenty-one-month period, Donna recorded more than 150 entries of unusual phenomena in her journals. Despite all that has happened at Rosemont, she said that she has never been afraid. "I think it's all positive energy," she theorized. "I can't explain all this, but I know in my heart there is nothing negative about it. If there are ghosts and they want to stay, that's fine with me. After all, they were here first."

COINCIDENCE OR FATE?

Three years after I had interviewed Donna Dean, who kept a diary of paranormal events at her house on Bent Mountain, I got a phone call from a woman named Stacy Beck in Alexandria. She wanted to tell me about the ghostly experiences she had as a child in a house—also on Bent Mountain just outside Roanoke. As her narrative went on, I got a really creepy feeling. It turns out she was describing the very same house that the Deans now owned, Rosemont. How's that for scary coincidence?

Stacy was just three years old when her family moved there in the 1960s, more than three decades before the Deans. Here's another curious twist: whereas Donna had never been afraid in the house and considered the spectral manifestations as "positive energy," Stacy had been badly frightened, either by the same or other residing spirits. "I was never comfortable there," she told me. Following are some excerpts of her testimony.

"So many things happened, from the basement to the attic," Stacy said. "One of the most terrifying things I remember was when I slept alone in the front bedroom. It was an old-fashioned bed with head- and footboards; the headboard was seven feet high. I would hear fingernails scraping all across the boards. The sounds then seemed to enter the wall and would continue there. Whenever I got scared, I would sleep in my parents' bedroom."

She continued. "The light switches were the kind you had to flip up or down. Several times, I actually saw a switch click on or off when no one was near it. Furniture would move. A rocking chair rocked on its own. Once, I saw a stationary chair slide all the way across a room. It was very disturbing. I didn't like going upstairs. I always felt like I was never alone up there. When I told my parents about all this, they just chalked it up to my imagination, but I knew it was real!" Stacy's mother later admitted that she, too, felt the house was haunted, but she didn't want to frighten her daughter anymore than she already was.

"The worst experience I had involved the door to the attic," Stacy said. "It always stuck and was hard to open. Sometimes, however, it would open on its own, so a special latch was put on it. Well, one night, I was alone in the house and had taken my clothes off to take a bath. All of a sudden, the latched attic door began to open. That was the fastest bath I ever took. I knew there was something there that was not of this world."

Twelve years after she moved out of the house, Stacy happened to be walking by it one evening when she said she heard a voice say, "Don't come back here!" No one was in sight. A few years later, she was in the area again and saw a for sale sign on the lawn. She walked up the side porch and saw a chair rocking with no one in it. "I got the weirdest feeling," she said, "and it was suddenly as cold as ice. This time I heard a woman's voice say, 'Go away! I know who you are.' I sensed it was a woman's spirit, and she didn't want me there. Why, I don't know."

There is a strange footnote here. Years earlier, when Stacy's family was living in Georgia, her mother, Chris, painted a picture of her imaginary dream house. Two years later, when they found the house on Bent Mountain, it was identical to the one she had envisioned in the painting. It was the same eerie experience Donna Dean had when she first saw the house.

Apparitions in Academia

One of the time-honored traditions at Hollins University, on the northern outskirts of Roanoke, is the telling of scary ghost stories to incoming students on or before Halloween week each year. The interesting thing about this practice is that according to scores of witnesses over the past century and a half, the stories are *true*. Some of the spirits encountered include Civil War soldiers and nurses.

Why? Well, the university itself predates that war. It was founded in 1842 and had a colorful history before that. Earlier, some of the buildings still used on campus today served as a boys' preparatory school, and before that, a resort hotel stood on the property, catering to guests who came far and wide to partake in the area's popular hot springs. During the Civil War, Hollins was closed, and its buildings were used as a Confederate hospital.

According to the university's website, Hollins's beginnings are synonymous with Charles Lewis Cocke, a young mathematics professor from Richmond who, at the age of nineteen, wrote that he wished to dedicate himself to "the upper education of women of the south." Cocke was not only credited as being the founder of the school, he was also a thinker far ahead of his time. During the middle of the nineteenth century, when the education of women was thought to be folly, even a possibly dangerous endeavor, he brazenly wrote, "The plan and policy of the school recognizes the principle that in the present state of society in our country young women require the same thorough and rigid training as that afforded to young men."

As one writer put it, "for decades, Hollins had a reputation as a place where wealthy southerners sent their daughters to learn French and painting,

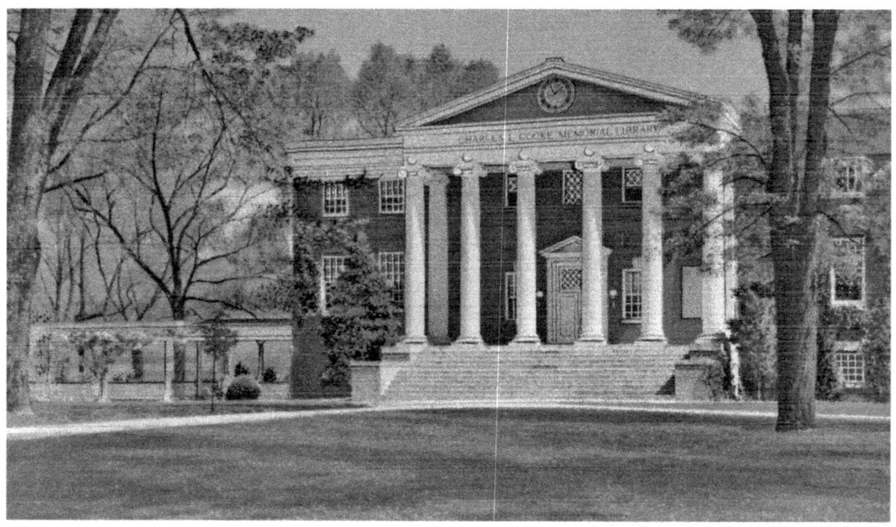

At Hollins College, incoming students are told tales of campus ghosts that are said to be true. *Asheville Card Company.*

while back home they looked for husbands for them." That thought has long since been erased. Today, the university is a leader in liberal arts and science education that offers, in a picturesque, small private college setting, an extensive undergraduate program for women, as well as distinguished coed graduate programs.

Although the administration strongly downplays it, Hollins also retains some ghostly figures from its distant past. There are, allegedly, several such spirits that haunt the dormitory hallways and campus walks. Their origins apparently range from the 1860s to the early 1900s.

One of the entities most frequently encountered is that of a former music student who tragically died in an automobile accident in the 1930s. Since then, many young women have experienced the sensation that someone is following them, but when they turn to see who it is, they catch only a fleeting glimpse and hear the swishing sounds of a longish skirt. One day a few years ago, a student and her faculty advisor were meeting in an office after classes had been closed. They both heard heavy footsteps approaching. The scary sounds stopped at the door to the office, and then the door began to shake violently. It badly frightened the two women, but when they finally managed the courage to open the door, there was no one in sight.

A prevailing legend concerns a music professor who fell in love with one of his students sometime in the late 1800s. When his advances were spurned, he killed himself. He has been said to return to the Presser Hall building, which houses the music library and practice rooms. Security watchmen occasionally have heard piano melodies coming from Presser in the dead of night, yet each time they check it out, there is nothing to be found. One young lady, working in the video lab one evening, noticed that the cords of the window blinds were going up and down on their own, and she got the distinct feeling that she was being watched by someone unseen. When she left the room and stepped into the unlighted hallway, she froze. There was a tall, dark male figure standing there. When it moved toward her, she panicked, burst through an outside door and ran. She heard footsteps behind her, which stopped only when she reached her dorm room.

Presser Hall, in fact, does seem to be the most haunted building on campus. Doors slam by themselves, and students have found themselves locked in a practice room that opened minutes later. A wedding or funeral procession has been witnessed entering and leaving the building. Associate professor of film Carl Plantings once said that a ghost has most recently been seen visiting video production students on the top floor of Presser. Two students saw a chair on wheels being flung across the floor by unseen hands, denting a register in an empty editing room. Another student felt a "wind" and looked behind her to see the figure of a man. He turned and floated down the stairs.

By far the saddest tradition told about Presser involved a young music student who fell in love with her piano professor, but they could never be together. Distraught, she reportedly cut her wrists and played the piano until she bled to death.

However, ghosts seem to be not confined to Presser Hall. The Hollins Theatre, for example, is believed to be the home of the spirit of "Elizabeth." The enduring rumor is that she committed suicide here in the 1920s and returns in apparition form, usually during play rehearsals, where she catches people off guard as she strolls across the stage or peeks out behind the lights.

Starkie House, now a residence hall, once served as the university infirmary. Here, students have told of being treated, when sick, by a strange nurse dressed in a uniform from another time. She has been sighted standing over bedridden young women and sometimes applies cool compresses to their heads. One student, grateful for the attention, went back to the infirmary to thank the head nurse for her treatment. She was told by the head nurse that no one had even entered her room.

In the Tinker dormitory, there have been a number of reports of sightings of Confederate soldiers walking the halls at night, and in more than one instance, these men were seen standing over startled young women in their beds.

In 2009, Ruth Carter, a contributor to Yahoo Notebook, visited the campus with her husband and a friend. When they tried to enter Presser Hall, they found the door locked. Minutes later, they saw that suddenly the door, strangely, was ajar. They walked down dark halls and then went upstairs, where Carter's friend took two consecutive photos. Carter said, "When my friend had her pictures developed, she noticed that the ones taken in the dark hallway were all lit up, and in the top of both photos was an unexplained strip of light that appeared to be moving upward. What was unsettling about these pictures was the fact that the light appeared to have moved within the split second between taking the pictures!"

And so the stories of Hollins's disembodied spirits are passed along, from classmate to classmate. But perhaps the most compelling incident involves the sighting of lights that flicker in the darkness over the small graveyard adjacent to the campus. The source of these lights has never been explained. But there is, perhaps, a telling clue. This is where Charles Lewis Cocke, the innovative founder of Hollins University, is buried.

A Closure at the Alms House

Just before Halloween 1995, I received a letter from Deborah Carvelli of Roanoke. She wrote, "I teach parapsychology at Virginia Western Community College. My class meets on Tuesdays and Thursdays. During this time the class picks up paranormal leads from the area, and we visit houses that want to tell a story." Following up, I called Deborah after talking to Louise Loveland, formerly with the Roanoke Historical Museum. Louise had been instrumental in developing a Halloween week tour of suspected haunted sites in the region. One of the places now annually visited is Virginia Western Community College. Deborah, it turns out, not only helped Louise set up this tour, but she has also often taken students to a particular building at the college, the Fine Arts Building, to study psychic phenomena there. This is what they had to report.

The building itself is old. At one time, it was used as an "Alms House." This was a place for the city's old, poor and disabled. There were reports that it was poorly run and that the residents were mistreated. One investigator said the house was not kept clean, was "filled with unsavory odors," and those living there were too afraid to complain.

Up the hill in back of the building was what was once known as the "Pest House." This was where the contagious sick, mostly those with dreaded smallpox, were sent. Old timers say that when the Alms House was filled, people were sent up to the Pest House, whether they were diseased or not.

The Alms House, in short, was a residence of misery. Many died there in uncomfortable and certainly unhappy circumstances. Some of the deaths may have been hastened by ill treatment and neglect. Perhaps for this reason, the building has long held the reputation of being haunted.

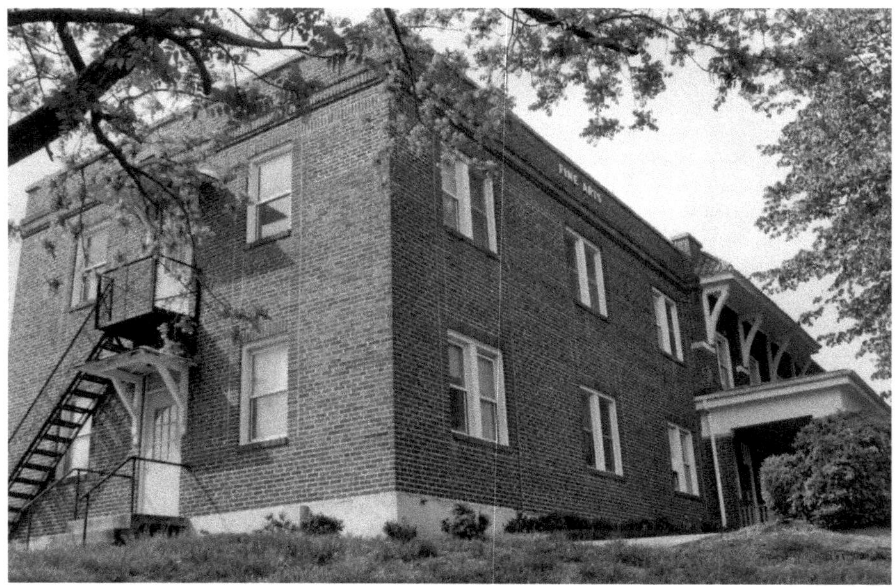

The Fine Arts Building, Virginia Western Community College (the Alms House), has long thought to be haunted. *Photo by the author.*

"There was a lot of human suffering here," Deborah said. "A lot of tragedy, and some of the residual stuff is still there. It's trapped energy. In fact, the whole land around here is strong in spiritual energy. Whenever I took my students in this building, they would pick right up on it. They felt the energy. It was like there was a powerful presence. Some of the students would even be overwhelmed by it. Some would cry. They could sense the sadness."

Specific manifestations, aside from the feelings of a presence, included lights that would be turned on at night when no one was there, unexplained noises at all hours of the evening and occasional glimpses of shadowy figures lurking about when no one was supposed to be on the premises. Such sensations have been experienced not only by Deborah's students on their visits but also by people who work in the Fine Arts Building.

Louise Loveland added that one of the most singular ghostly manifestations occurred just outside the building, where a huge old oak tree, since removed, once stood. "When we went out to set up the site for our haunting tour, we talked to the security policemen there," she said. "They had some stories to tell. One officer said that he had an encounter that made his hair stand on end. He said one night he and another policeman were making their rounds of the college, and when they pulled into a driveway, they saw a man standing there. It was at night, and everyone had gone for the day, so there shouldn't have been anyone there. They said there was something 'odd' about the man. They wondered why he was there, so they stopped and asked if they could help him."

"He didn't speak," Louise continued. "He just laughed and gestured to the big tree with his hand. They asked him again, and he repeated the gesture. His attitude seemed strange. They thought he might be drunk. One officer got an uneasy feeling and suggested to the other to let the man go, but the other officer told him to wait a minute. This officer then reached out to grab the man, and his hand went right through him! Then the figure suddenly disappeared before their eyes."

"The next day, something else strange happened. The two officers went back to the tree. One of them had a theory that the answer to the mysterious apparition they had both seen had something to do with the tree. So one policeman grabbed a shovel and started to dig around the base of the tree," Louise added. "He put his foot on the top of the shovel head and shoved it down into the earth. It stuck. He couldn't get the shovel out of the ground. Both men tried, but no matter how hard they strained, the shovel wouldn't budge. Finally, they tied a rope to the shovel and attached it to the back of their vehicle and had to pull it out that way. After that, they didn't bother with the tree anymore."

Early in February 1997, Deborah took a class of her students to the building. "I have always believed that timing is so important," she said. "They were just about to do some major renovations there. They were going to convert the area inside into offices, so the students and I wanted to try and alleviate any spirits still trapped there. We did an energy circle. That's where we all sit in a circle, hold hands and try to send positive feelings and universal love inside."

"It must have worked, because we all got a feeling of total transition," she noted. "We all visualized something was happening. It was like there was a great release. We were, in effect, saying to the spirits that it was okay to move on, and there was a definite feeling that flight was opening up. We all felt that we had been heard and understood, and that a heavy presence had been lifted. It felt wonderful."

A Passel of Paranormal Vignettes

Here is an assortment of abbreviated accounts of suspected ghostly activity in and around Roanoke.

Plantation Phenomena

Bellevue Plantation, located on Old Mountain Road, was built in 1854 and was then known as the Kyle Hotel. It later served as a private residence and as a school for the disabled. That history might help explain the psychic activity that owner Linda Selfe has experienced there. In 1994, she told *Roanoke Times* staff writer Crystal Chappell that she often heard footsteps in the house when no one else was home, as well as the sounds of a child running up and down the stairs, hitting the rungs of the banister with a stick. It was enough for her to declare that she would never spend another night in Bellevue alone.

Rendezvous in Roanoke

About twenty years ago, William Goodlett, then an octogenarian, taught art at the Salem Senior Citizens Center. Once, he had a guest from Oregon. She said that she saw the ghost Goodlett had often heard and felt at his house on Union Street in Roanoke. She added that she awoke in the middle of a dark and stormy night because she felt as if someone was standing beside her bed. It was the apparition of a woman, who quickly evaporated before her eyes.

Goodlett knew what she was talking about because he had encountered the spirit a number of times over the years. He claimed that "she" had tucked him into bed on occasion, patted his shoulders once and honked a horn on a shelf in the closet. He believed it might be the spectral return of Anna Marion Brand, whose husband, W. Lee Brand, built the house more than a century ago. Goodlett said that Mrs. Brand died in Maryland in 1931, but her spirit wasn't content until she could return to her beloved home after her death.

A SMOKY RETREAT

No smoking is allowed at the Old Manse Bed-and-Breakfast in Salem, but guests say that someone must be cheating because they distinctly smell cigarette smoke there on occasion. It may be caused by a former inhabitant, long since dead. The house, at 530 East Main Street, was built in 1847 by John Day, a blacksmith. It later served, until 1939, as a residence for Presbyterian ministers. Old Manse is listed on the National Historic Register, and guests today are treated with a full southern breakfast.

The mystery smoke, however, isn't the only strange phenomenon. Lights sometimes turn on and off by themselves, although the house has been completely rewired, and electricians could find no rational cause for this. For some unexplained reason, it mostly happens near shelves of books. Heavy doors also open and close with no obvious cause, and occasionally, between 2:00 and 3:00 a.m., an unmistakable *thud* is heard, the significance of which is unknown.

What or who causes all this? Owner Charlotte Griffith is not sure, but she remembered a former resident who liked to smoke while reading in bed.

THE TIDY GHOST

The following was contributed anonymously on the Internet by a former pilot for a southern regional airline.

A few years ago we had a stopover in a Roanoke hotel. It was to be a short layover and when one of the flight attendants entered her room, exhausted, she just flung her uniform on the bed and undressed. While reading a book, she said she felt the room was suddenly cold, then she felt a "weight" at the bottom of her bed. She looked up and saw an old woman with scraggly hair, in a nightgown, standing there.

For some reason she said she wasn't immediately scared, but felt saddened at the sight. She closed her eyes and when she reopened them, the figure had vanished. This did frighten her and she raced down to the lobby and asked the night clerk to come with her back to her room. Curiously, he refused. He bluntly said the room was haunted; that there had been other reports of the old woman's appearance.

Upset, the flight attendant spent the night in the lobby. The next morning she reported the incident to a hotel security officer. When they went up to her room, she was astonished to find her crumpled uniform carefully smoothed out and folded, as if it had been freshly pressed. Then she looked into her wallet. She had wadded up some paper money from alcohol sales on the flight and stuffed it into her purse, planning to sort it out later. She found the bills all neatly folded, and in ranking denominations, ones, fives, etc., all with the faces in order!

Later, it was learned that the hotel had once been an assisted living facility for the elderly. The woman who had lived in this particular room had no family and told her attending nurse that she had willed her all the money she had. Apparently, the nurse couldn't wait. She killed the old woman!

TAVERN TERROR

At the Blackhorse Tavern, a former ghost tour guide said on her first visit there that it felt like the breath was being sucked out of her. Past tenants and caretakers have told of hearing "tavern-like noises" and people clomping up and down the stairs late at night. It is reported that there is a great deal of psychic activity in the oldest section of the building, and that may be the reason no one seemed to be able to stay in the house very long. Many people have moved here and then moved out again within days or weeks. Also, according to some local ghost investigative groups, there is a longstanding tradition of the sighting of a man on a white horse riding from this site toward the town of Hollins. The general belief is that he is searching for his long-lost love.

THE HAUNTING HERMIT

Roanoke ghost tour operators say that they once looked into a colorful legend that has been passed down from generation to generation of an old hermit who lived in a cave on nearby Read Mountain. The story is that a century or so ago, he was a tinker who fixed pots and pans and other metal things. He was, however, rarely seen in public and only would come down from the mountain every few months for supplies. When this was researched, people in the area said that the apparition of the hermit is still seen walking down the mountain. Several years ago, someone found some evidence of what may have been his haunt. Several pieces of old tin were scattered around in a cave.

THE CLOSED DOOR INCIDENT

At the Roanoke Library Bookfest in November 2001, I met a most engaging young man named Ervin Jordon Jr. He was an associate professor at the University of Virginia. He told me the following episode.

This happened about forty years ago, when I was five years old. We were having a family reunion at one of my granduncle's farms, and there were many children there. I remember I was playing with a girl I would guess was about my age. She had on kind of a funny dress in that it was old and raggedy, and looking back on it, I would say it probably was from another, earlier era. But being so young myself, I really didn't think about it at the time. We were just playing and having a good time.

We decided to explore my granduncle's old house. We started walking around, and we went into a long, darkened hallway. There was only a single light bulb shining. We got to a closed door. I tried to open it, but it wouldn't budge. So I said to the girl, "We can't go in there. The door is locked."

She looked at me and smiled. She said, "You can't go in, but I can!" And then she walked *through* the door! She didn't open it and walk in; she went through the door! I recall standing there, stunned. For some reason, I wasn't afraid, but I just didn't understand how she did that.

I ran into the kitchen, where my parents and others had gathered, and told them what I had just seen happen. It got dead quiet in an instant. I was told to shush and go outside. To this day, my mother steadfastly refuses to discuss the incident.

THE CORPSE THAT SHOUTED "DON'T SHOOT!"

In October 1998, the Virginia Museum of Transportation in Roanoke held its first-ever "Haunted Railroad" tour during Halloween week. Education director Judy Hensley said that she had no idea of what to expect. As it turned out, she was overwhelmed. More than 360 people showed up. One of the incidents recounted on the tour was rather humorous. It seems that in 1886, a crook dreamed up a novel scheme. He concealed himself on an express train leaving the city by hiding himself in a coffin! The plan was to extricate himself from the box along the route and then rob the train.

A rail agent, however, either alertly or perhaps scared to death, foiled the attempt. He heard noise coming from the coffin. It is conceivable that he may have believed someone was coming back from the dead. Whatever the reason, he piled some heavy freight on top of the casket, and when it arrived at the next station, the agent had it placed on the platform. He then yelled, "If anyone is in there, you'd better come out, or I'm going to shoot through the lid"

A sheepish voice inside suddenly cried out, "Don't shoot! I'm in here." The chagrined, would-be bandit was promptly arrested, tried in court and sentenced to a three-year prison term.

A LIFESAVING WARNING

There is no mention of the appearance of a werewolf in the Roanoke police records of 1970. On the afternoon of August 22, 1970, three young children, aged eleven and twelve, two boys and a girl, were playing in the wooded area behind their homes when they came upon an abandoned construction shack. Poking around on the dirt floor, they found an old wooden box filled with sticks of dynamite. The kids didn't recognize the danger of their discovery and thought they were fireworks.

They decided to set them off, but they had no matches, so they went back home for some, returning at dusk. When they found no fuses, they piled the sticks together and surrounded them with dry leaves, intending to set fire to the leaves. But just before they lit the matches, they heard a rustling sound nearby. Someone was approaching.

Emerging from the edge of the woods was what they described as a figure the size of a tall man, but it wasn't a man. It looked more like a wild animal.

It had a hairy face with red eyes, and its open mouth exposed fangs! One of the children, terrified, screamed, "It's a werewolf!" As it approached the shack, the three ran as fast as they could to a nearby highway.

A police car happened to be passing by, and the officers stopped to warn the children not to run on the road. They then stammered to the police that a werewolf had tried to grab them. They led the officers to the shack and were told they had been extremely lucky they had been frightened off; had they lit the fire, the explosion of dynamite would have blown them to pieces.

As to the children's story of the werewolf, the officers were, of course, highly skeptical—that is, until they found footprints near the shack in the shape of a large wolf's paws.

An Uncomfortable House

In his big 1968 book *The History of the City of Roanoke*, author Raymond Barnes cited events that occurred year by year. In 1892, he quoted a newspaper account as follows: "There was, and perhaps still is, a house in the city reliably reported to be haunted. A person by the name of Carrie Lee died in a house on 5th Ave, S.E. Every tenant that rented the house after her death later returned to the agent's office vowing that a dark woman was seen about the premises at night. Neither Negro or white could be persuaded to stay in the place."

The Pallbearers' Plea

In the year 1900, a newspaper report was published regarding a longstanding tradition in Roanoke. Protest was heard, supposedly at a town meeting, about the custom of expecting pallbearers at funerals to fill in graves with dirt. Bearers of the deceased dressed in their best out of respect for the departed. Yet regardless of the weather, pallbearers were expected to handle a shovel and possibly ruin their clothing. There was no word as to when this custom was abandoned.

THE MAN WHO SAID HE COULD FLY

In 1900, an itinerant African American preacher from North Carolina named William McKinley held a series of revival meetings in Roanoke that many attended with fervor. At one of these, McKinley became so "worked up" and enthusiastic that he announced that he was "going to soar away." Climbing up to the second floor of a building, he spread his arms and jumped, only to fall flat on his back in an alley. He then embarrassingly announced that the time for him to fly had not yet arrived.

THE RESTLESS TODDLER

For a long time, Roanoke neighbors Pernela Turner and Vicki Fox were afraid to talk about it, especially to each other, for fear of being thought crazy. Pernela had been hearing "rattling" sounds and loud bangs emanating from the kitchen, but she could never pin down the source. Her sister, Linda Hobson, who also lived in the house, reported hearing "a spirit" calling her name. Meanwhile, next door, Vicki and others of her family were experiencing similar manifestations, including unexplained visions. She even had her pastor come to her house and rub the sign of the cross into her walls with anointing oil.

Then, one day, a possible cause for the phenomena was uncovered, literally. Moochie, Pernela's dog, dug up a century-old tombstone in the backyard right along the fence line that separated her house with Vicki's. It was a tiny stone and read, cryptically, "Ironton 1780–1." Archaeologist Mike Barber was called in, and he said that the information indicated that the stone marked the grave of a one-year-old child, and it probably had been part of a small family cemetery. He didn't know what "Ironton" meant. Additional research seemed to show that the child could have been kin to a Lord Ironton of England, who settled in southwest Virginia more than two hundred years ago.

Historian Clare White, associated with the Roanoke Valley History Museum, suggested that since the grave was found only a short distance from the Wilderness Road, a trail many settlers followed into Kentucky, the child might have died as a family forged west.

Both Pernela and Vicki, who compared notes once the grave was discovered, believed that they had found the answers to all the strange things that happened in their houses. After the stone was recovered, and since Moochie was kept away from it, the odd occurrences ceased.

DEATH TIMES FIVE

Eunice Anderson of Vinton, on the eastern outskirts of Roanoke, told of an electrifying experience her mother, Helen, once had when she was thirteen years old. She was babysitting for her sister one night when, all of a sudden, an old clock that hadn't worked in five years began to chime. It struck five times. Helen had never heard it strike before and was petrified. She grabbed her niece and ran out of the house.

Shortly afterward, when she went back in, the telephone rang. Helen was told that there had been a bad accident. Her brother and five others had been struck in their car by a train. Her brother had survived, but the five other people had all been killed. It was later learned that the accident had occurred at the precise time the old clock had struck. It had tolled five times—one for each fatality.

"DOC" PINKARD'S DARK SECRETS

What was it about Doc Pinkard's old house that scared so many people? There was an overwhelming, eerie feeling years ago at 4347 Franklin Road in Roanoke in a converted house that was built in the 1920s. It later became an art and antique gallery, but there was an unpleasant aura that seemed to linger from bygone days. Customers noticed it while browsing in the shop, and some old-time neighbors steadfastly refused to enter the place, even in the daylight. Of course, the house and shop are no longer there—they were razed a few years ago for a new Lowe's store. Still, the paranormal rumors persist.

Longtime residents were convinced that the house was haunted. And there are a number of reported manifestations seen by several witnesses to back up such a claim. Tom Davis said that he first heard about it when he bought the house in 1972. He added that an old man walked up to him one day outside the building and told him, "I'm standing as close to it as I'll ever come to it. It's haunted! I've heard the most awful moaning coming from it." Then the old man walked off.

"Older people in the area wouldn't come in here," said George Ferguson, who bought the art gallery from Davis. "They'd stand outside and talk to you, but they wouldn't come inside. They said I was crazy for coming in here." Ferguson said that he has heard strange and unaccountable noises inside the house—noises he has investigated and found no rational source for.

Others, too, have had weird experiences in the former house-shop. There was, for example, the instance of the disappearing customer. Davis said that when he ran the business, he saw a man enter the gallery many times, but when he would turn to help him, the man was gone. He had no idea where he went. Ferguson had the same thing happen to him.

Customers spoke of unnatural "vibes" coming from the upstairs section, and a man once told Davis that he had seen another person literally evaporate as he stared at him. According to Davis, the man said, "That man didn't move forward or backward. He just went *poof*." Davis added that the man who told him this had goose bumps all up and down his arms. "I don't believe in ghosts," said Davis. "I probably was just not being observant enough, but I don't know how you explain things like that."

Roanoke Times staff writer Christina Nickols wrote a Halloween article about the house in October 1997. For background material, she talked to Loyd Aurbach, director of the Office of Paranormal Investigations in San Francisco. He told her, based on what she had uncovered in her interviews, that the house may not have been actually haunted. He said that real spirits tend to be a lot more rambunctious than the passive apparitions that had been sighted at the gallery. Instead, he believed that what customers had seen were "imprints" of past events and dead people that can still be experienced at later dates. "It's more like a recording," Aurbach said. He told Nickols that such imprints often occur in areas with a high magnetic field, and the fact that iron ore was once mined in the region was a clue that such a field could exist.

But if the entities heard and seen were imprints, ghosts or whatever, who and what were they and why were they there? Old-timers in the area all deeply believe that they were associated with the first resident of the house, a curious and charismatic man named John Henry Pinkard, affectionately known as "Doc" Pinkard.

In the 1920s and early 1930s (he died in 1934), Doc operated a flourishing herbal medicine business in the house. Whether he was a certified doctor is not known, but it is generally believed that he wasn't. Nevertheless, it is true that many Roanoke natives, from all walks of life, sought Pinkard out for treatments. He had a house full of jugs of alcohol, which he mixed with herbs to sell as remedies for everything from the common cold to asthma. Over time, he became known as a popular "yarb" (herb) doctor.

Perhaps adding to the odd atmosphere of the house was the fact that Doc Pinkard was, in a word, strange. It is said that he once constructed a fence of hollow ceramic jugs that made an "awesome howl" when the wind blew. Some were convinced that he did this to frighten neighborhood children who climbed into his apple trees in season and made off with the fruit. But others think he did this just to scare off curious onlookers who tried to peer in his windows and see what kind of homemade concoctions he was brewing. Among them were his "Sanguinaria and Hydrastic Compounds" and his "Great Liniment"—all laced liberally with alcohol.

Who are the apparitions or imprints that remained behind when the gallery was in operation? "We heard a lot of footsteps there at times when we knew no one else was in the house," said Ferguson. "We always said that's just old Doc Pinkard." However, many longtime residents contend that the old house was haunted by former patients. They said that some of these people went into the house and never came out. One man told Tom Davis when he bought the place in 1972 that customers who had been treated by Doc were buried in the basement.

Roanoke's Conjuror

Doc Pinkard was preceded in Roanoke by another alleged doctor. His name was W.H. Reavis. City historian Raymond Barnes described the scene in 1905 this way:

> *Negroes were a constant prey to quacks, conjure men, herb doctors and jokers. "Doctor" Reavis carried a little black bag, such as physicians carried. Not only did he prescribe and administer medicines, but he also was a juggler, a necromancer, horoscope caster, star gazer, prestidigitator, fortune teller, and master of several other arts by which he preyed on the ignorant. His activities continued well up into World War I days.*

By the Grave's Early Light

Among the most revered heroes in the greater Roanoke area was a brooding military genius who was described by biographers as being witty, ambitious, self-reliant, unbearably acidic, unquestionably loyal and aggressively bold. Robert E. Lee hailed him as a determined, resourceful and energetic leader. This was Jubal Early, general, Confederate States of America, a champion of the Southern cause and a man who went to his grave in 1894, wearing a gray suit and cuff links imprinted with the Confederate flag. He was a native of the Red River section of Franklin County, Virginia, a few miles southeast of Roanoke, where his father operated a thriving plantation.

One might consider that Jubal Early had just cause to return to his home region in spirit form and continue to lead phantom charges, because he did, after all, spend the last thirty years of his life seeking a justification for the Southern secession and an explanation for the ultimate defeat of his beloved Confederacy.

However, it is not his ghostly form that has been sighted roaming across isolated, long-deserted cemeteries in the Burnt Chimney region of the county. It is, rather, the specter of his brother, William Early, who continues a spectral search for his life's savings, which disappeared from his grave in a bizarre manner 150 or so years ago.

William Early's nocturnal ventures manifest themselves as a strange light that has been seen (but never explained) by hundreds of witnesses over several generations. "Many people have seen it," said local historian

Gertrude Mann, "but nobody knows what it is." Some believe it to be the gentle golden light of Early's lantern as his spirit wanders restlessly from tombstone to tombstone, searching for his lost treasure.

The legend has an intriguing origin. William Early died in the mid-1860s and was buried with his money beside him. Just why his wife and children allowed this has never been known. Perhaps they were unaware of it, and curiously, he may have thought that you really could take it with you.

Nevertheless, in time his widow fell in love with the family farm's overseer, and they decided to get married. This appalled Mrs. Early's children, who felt that their mother was lowering herself in society. So they decided to take matters into their own hands. As one newspaper reporter wrote, "They decided to stop the wedding with the help of an uninvited guest." It was deemed that drastic measures were necessary, and their macabre actions were shocking to say the least.

William Early's sons went to their father's grave, dug up the coffin and carried it back to the farmhouse. There, they stood the glass-covered coffin upright at the base of the stairs to greet their mother when she descended the steps in her wedding gown. Alas, the eerie plot did not work. Mrs. Early defiantly strode past the corpse and walked into the parlor, where the marriage then took place. Chagrined, the sons reburied the remains of the father in another grave site, the exact location of which is today unknown. Somehow in the process, William Early's money was either lost or stolen.

Ever since then, Early's light has been sighted dancing across remote grave sites from the Burnt Chimney section all the way to the Roanoke County line. Many have seen the light dart about in the inky darkness. Others have chased it, seeking a sane and sensible solution to its appearances. No one has succeeded.

Some longtime residents dismiss the light as being caused by swarms of fireflies, but there are no fireflies in the dead of winter. Some have said that it is the light of hunters' lanterns, but no hunters have ever stepped forward to justify this possibility. It is, say old-timers, the ghostly light of William Early, Jubal Early's brother, who cannot rest in peace until he finds his money, lost more than a century and a half ago.

A Host of Haunting Humor

Quite often, when unexplained events occur, there is a quick perception that a ghost is involved. Sometimes, this is proven false when a rational answer to the phenomenon is found. Every once in a while, such situations prove to be downright humorous. Following are some true examples of this, all collected from Roanoke and the surrounding area.

A Headless Non-Ghost

Dewey Plaster, a Roanoke native, has been fascinated with the paranormal all his life. He said that he was most frightened when he was a young boy visiting his grandmother and had a scary encounter with a closet. "When I opened the door," he recalls, "I saw a headless woman." He screamed. "Out the bedroom door, down the hall, through the kitchen and out the back door I went, flying! I told Grandma there was a headless ghost in her closet." Dewey was stunned when she laughed out loud. She then walked him back into the room, opened the closet door and showed him…a cloth mannequin.

RETURN OF A DEAD HUSBAND

During the latter years of the Great Depression, the Works Progress Administration hired writers to fan across Virginia and record oral histories and folklore. This account was filed by Gertrude Blair, who interviewed "Minnie the cook" on June 9, 1939, in Roanoke. It is recounted here by permission of the Blue Ridge Institute in Ferrum, Virginia.

> *While I was in the kitchen of the house where I live, the other day, Minnie was in a talkative mood. She told several stories of "hants" coming in her room, and of a recent visit by her husband, who died several years ago. There is no power that would ever shake her belief in "hants."*
>
> *Well, she said that before the Yale lock was put on her door, her husband paid her a visit in the dead hours of the night. When she awoke, she claimed he was standing by her bed, looking down at her. Minnie said he looked just as "natrall."*
>
> *I said, "why Minnie, didn't it scare you half to death?" "No," she answered, "I jes say, 'Jim, for heaven's sake, what is you doin' here?' He says, 'Minnie, I's come for you.' I told him, 'When the Lord's ready for me, He'll come. He won't send you.' I ain't seen him no more."*

A QUESTION OF FAITH

The following is extracted from the old *Confederate Veteran* magazine. During the Civil War, when Union soldiers were approaching Roanoke, a squad of troops found an elderly woman in a log cabin one day. One of them asked her, "Well, old lady are you a secessionist?" "No," she replied. The soldier next inquired if she was a Unionist, and again she said no. "What are you then?" she was asked. "A Baptist," she said, "and always have been"

A FUNERAL MOST EXPENSIVE

The source for this anecdote is unknown, lost in time. However, it has been told and retold in and around Roanoke for more than three quarters of a century. Seems about seventy-five or so years ago, there were two young brothers living on a farm outside of the city. When they were grown, one went off to seek his fortune in the corporate world and made it big. The other brother stayed home with his father and worked the farm.

One day, the wealthy one got a telegram from his brother saying their father had died and that the funeral would be held in two days. He wired back that he would not be able to attend, but he said to give their father the very best funeral possible and to send the bill to him. He would pay for everything.

A week or so later, this brother got a bill for $5,000, which he promptly settled. A month later came another bill, for $100. He paid that, too, thinking something had been forgotten. Then, when he got more bills for $100 the next two months, he called his brother on the farm and asked him what they were for.

His brother said, "Well, you wanted Papa buried in style, so I rented him a tuxedo!"

THE CORPSE THAT ATE A POTATO

There is an old African American folk tale concerning the death of one of the elder members of a family who lived in a log cabin in a rural area just outside Roanoke. One evening, as the newly departed gentleman laid peacefully in his coffin in the main room of the cabin, family members were "sitting up with the dead," the time-honored tradition of the wake. They had put some potatoes to roast on the fire, but as it was late at night, they had fallen asleep.

By chance, two hunters came upon the place, perhaps drawn by the smoke from the chimney. They peered through a window, and being famished, they quickly devised a diabolical plan. They slipped into the cabin and stole the potatoes. Before they left, however, they set the head and shoulders of the deceased man up in the coffin, pried his mouth open and put one of the potatoes in it. Then they snuck outside and looked again through the window, waiting to see what happened when the others woke up.

The first person awoke, stretched and looked back toward the body. He then let out the most bloodcurdling scream and shouted, "Grandpa done come to and eat up all the potatoes! There he sits with one in his mouth!" He then lit out of the cabin as fast as his legs would carry him. The others, aroused, followed in close pursuit.

The last one out, however, in his haste, caught his suspenders on the door latch, which had a hook on it. Fearing that he had been grabbed by the corpse, he fainted dead away. It was quite some time before any of the others went back to check on him.

CEMETERY CREEPINESS

In November 1927, a picture framer from Roanoke was accused of robbing a prohibition officer of his badge, pistol and a pint of whiskey. When a warrant was sworn out for the man, the officer was deemed to be drunk and was warned not to seek the arrest until the next day. But he went after his assailant anyway, along with a friend. When they overtook the man, a fight ensued, and he was shot with the very pistol he had been accused of stealing.

They brought him to a local doctor, but he died before making a statement, perhaps because he had been shot in the mouth. Both the officer and his friend were indicted for murder, but they were found not guilty. The victim's body lay unclaimed in the morgue for some time, until his wife and father finally showed up to identify him. Strangely, they left town without telling anyone what to do with the body. He was eventually buried in a donated cemetery space.

Apparently, however, the alleged thief could not rest easily; several townspeople have seen a mysterious figure lurking in the graveyard late at night. It seems to evaporate when approached. Perhaps it is the Roanoke man, seeking retribution for the fact that he was unable to speak for himself in this controversial case.

At the Tazewell Avenue Cemetery in Roanoke, the apparition of an old woman has been seen sitting on a wall surrounding a family burial plot. The local legend is that she died during the great flu epidemic in 1918. Her husband and children survived her, and when they passed on, they were buried in this plot. The woman's wraith has been witnessed there, crying, because (allegedly) she wasn't ready to leave her family so unexpectedly.

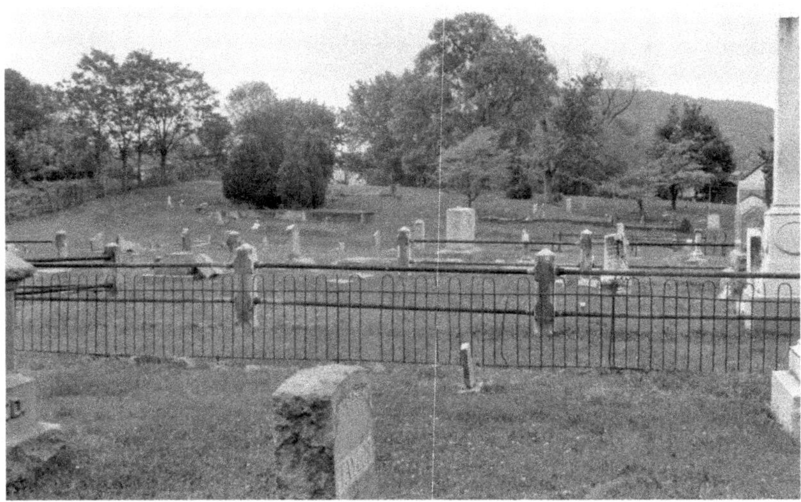

Tazewell City Cemetery. The apparition of a sad old woman crying has been sighted here. *Photos by the author.*

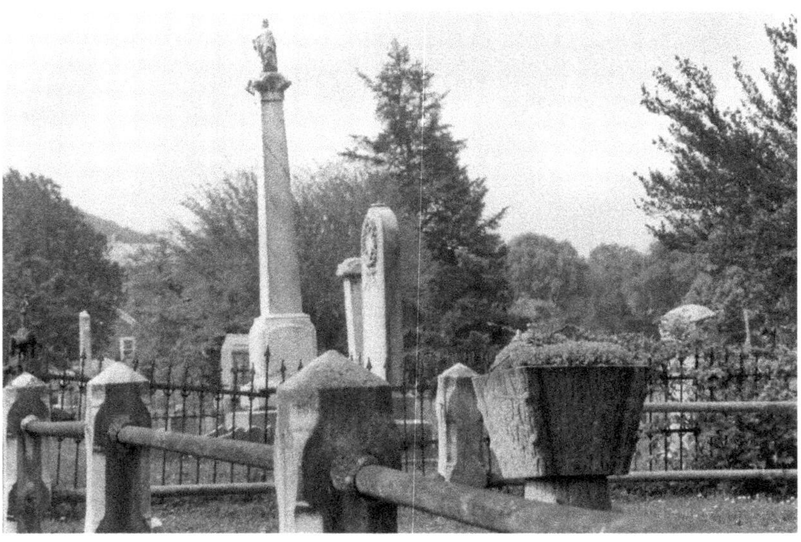

Louise Loveland, formerly with the city's history museum, said that a tour guide and the visitors got an unexpected thrill on the night of the 1996 annual Roanoke ghost tour. "While we were there, in the midst of telling this story, a solid white cat appeared out of nowhere and leaped up on the very headstone we were facing," Louise recalled. "There were quite a few audible gasps."

The Highwayman Who Saw the Light

Two centuries ago, those who chose to settle in the Roanoke area—and all over southwest Virginia, for that matter—were constantly being threatened, not only by marauding Indians but also by dangerous highwaymen. These renegade bandits would hide along popular trails and ambush anyone traveling by: cattle drovers, stagecoach passengers and lone horseback riders, all of whom were robbed and, in most cases, left stranded in the barren, remote wilderness.

One of the most colorful, charismatic and swashbuckling of such rogues was a man named Joseph Thompson Hare. For more than twenty years, his criminal exploits were well known from New Orleans to Canada, yet he reached legendary status not only for his daringly bold holdups but also for his fierce Indian fighting, his uncanny ability to outwit and escape from the law and his bare-handed killing of a panther that attacked him. There was also a benevolent side to Hare, and this gained him a reputation as being an American Robin Hood. He often gave victims back enough of their money so that they wouldn't be left destitute and isolated—a rather peculiar twist for a man in his profession.

In the early 1800s, Hare received a letter from a friend inviting him to come to Richmond. Riding up from the south, he fell in with a drover also heading that way, and just outside what is now Roanoke, Hare decided to rob his companion. He did, but then he was struck with strange pangs of remorse. Hare later described what happened next:

> *I cannot account for the extraordinary feelings which had seized possession of me, unless it was a warning from some mysterious and supernatural power. I felt like a man under the influence of some hideous nightmare, and every time I*

urged my beast to speed, it seemed to me as if a crowd of fiends were whistling in my course, and on the point of laying their avenging grasp upon my shoulder.

Then a thing occurred, from the recollection of which I shrink, even in this dreadful hour. The moon had risen during my flight and was bright and full. I had been galloping through a long stretch of narrow road, the bordering trees of which shut out her beams, and left the surface of the path in gloom.

Suddenly I emerged into an open rise, and there, in the moon's silvery light, stood, right across the road, a pure white horse—immovable as marble, and so white that it almost seemed to be radiating light. I was startled by the first glance at the apparition, but expecting it to give way, I pressed towards it. But it did not stir, but stood with its small graceful head stretched out, its tail slightly raised, as if in a listening attitude, and its ears cocked sharply forward and strained towards the moon, on which its gaze seemed to be unwaveringly fixed. When within almost six feet of it, my horse suddenly recoiled upon its haunches, and, opening his nostrils with affright, gave a short cry of terror, and attempted to turn around.

I trembled in my saddle as if struck with a sudden ague, but not daring to return into the gloom behind, I closed my eyes, bent my head, and driving my sharp heels deep into my horse's side, pressed forward at the fearful object. My steed took but one plunge and then landed on its fore-feet, firmly resolved not to budge another inch. I opened my eyes, and the apparition had disappeared. But an instant had elapsed and no trace of it was left. My most superstitious terrors were then confirmed, and I feared to go forward over the charmed space where the strange figure had stood.

I have been told that I was laboring under a state of mental hallucination that night; an illusion super induced by a peculiar state of nervous agitation, and that these things were mere chimeras of a feverish brain; but I know better!

Stunned by the encounter, Hare retreated to an inn he had passed adjacent to the Roanoke settlement; he was captured there later that night by a band of men, friends of the robbed drover. One of Hare's biographers wrote, "The specter was present to his sense, and having terrified him from a sure escape and delivered him into the hands of his pursuers, may be recognized as the supernatural decider of his fate."

Hare was convicted of this crime and served five years in the state penitentiary. He then said, still awed by the paranormal vision he had encountered, that he "saw the folly of a career in crime" and repented. "I resolved to live honestly for the future," he vowed. But, alas, temptation overtook him again. Caught robbing a stagecoach carrying U.S. mail, he was sentenced to death and was hanged on the morning of September 10, 1818.

Watchdog of the Valley Frontier

It used to be said, early in the twentieth century, that when the winds whipped up at old Greenfield Mansion near Daleville, west of Troutville and in the northern suburbs of Roanoke, that the "God-awful" noises of heavy boot stomping and loud banging doors were made by the ghost of Colonel William Preston. The entity, it was believed, appeared to maintain a spectral watch over the spirits of marauding Indians who continued to threaten the peace of early valley settlers two and a half centuries after the colonel had fought them off in real life.

Above all else, William Preston was an Indian fighter. He was so dedicated to the protection of his fellow Virginians, in fact, that he once turned his own house into a fortress haven for men, women and children seeking shelter against enemy attacks. His fierce resolve and determination earned him the title "Watchdog of the Virginia Frontier."

Preston was born in Donegal, Ireland, in 1739 and was eight years old when his father brought the family to America. His father died when he was a teenager, and he went to live with his uncle, Colonel James Patton. Patton was killed during an Indian raid at Draper's Meadow, south of Roanoke, in 1755, and young Preston was spared only because he had been sent to a neighboring farm to solicit help in harvesting. This event deeply saddened him and helped foster his lifelong pursuit of revenge.

In the late 1750s, Preston bought several hundred acres of land near the hamlet of Amsterdam and built a house known as Greenfield. It was constructed on a hill to provide a long-range panoramic view of the

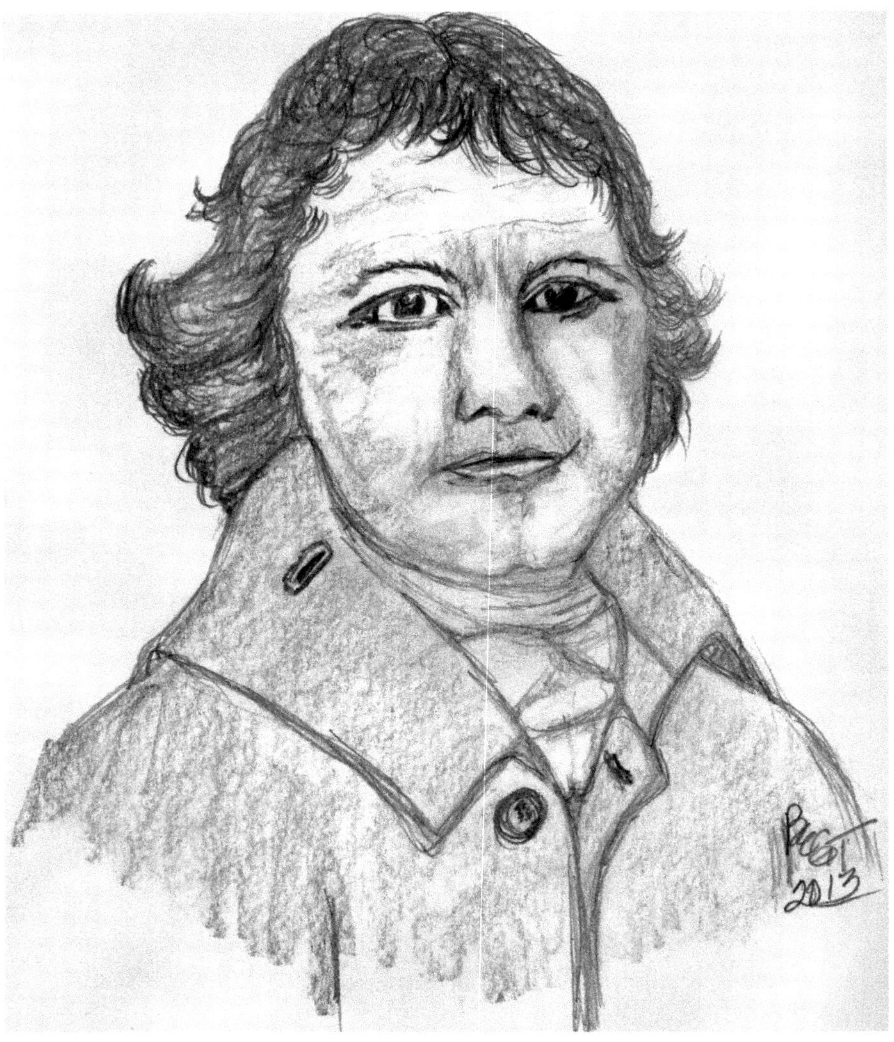

The ghost of Colonel William Preston is said to haunt old Greenfield Mansion near Daleville, outside Roanoke. *Illustration by Brenda E. Goens.*

surrounding countryside. One wing featured tall columns and was erected as a combination log house and fort for defense against Indians.

He chose the site and design wisely. In a letter he wrote in the mid-eighteenth century, he described the Indians as "being on the warpath" and added that within the walls of Greenfield were "80 men, 40 guns, and by the grace of God" he hoped to hold the fort. Biographers have written that Colonel Preston "was almost constantly engaged in either leading or preparing for expeditions against the Indians. During the Revolutionary War he was not only active in defending the outposts of southwest Virginia against the Indians, but also in fighting the British Loyalists in their attempts to foment trouble."

Meanwhile, more additions were added to the house on top of the hill, and Greenfield began to assume a revered position as a historic landmark. George Washington came here during one of his last surveying trips to the frontier before the outbreak of the Revolutionary War. Colonel Preston either knew or corresponded with most of the colonial leaders of the day, including Patrick Henry, Richard Henry Lee, Lord Botetourt and Lord Dunmore.

Having survived a lifetime of danger, dodging British muskets and Indian arrowheads and tomahawks, the crusty old warrior died as he might have wished it, at a regimental muster held near his home, on June 18, 1783. He left quite a legacy. Eight generations of the Preston family lived at Greenfield. The estate included nearly one thousand acres, vast apple orchards, a large herd of cattle and thoroughbred horses.

After his death, Greenfield also housed a noisy ghost. So prevalent were the rumors that the mansion was haunted by the avenging specter of the colonel, ever vigilant in his guard against Indian attacks, that Preston descendants had a hard time hiring help to run the house and estate. Servants were wary of being in the mansion, especially after dark, for it was in the wee hours of the evening, particularly on windy nights, that the manifestations most often occurred. "He" was said to stomp about on the upstairs floors, opening and slamming doors. His grandchildren and great-grandchildren would search the entire upstairs to find a plausible explanation for the sounds, never to succeed. It was, some said, Colonel Preston making his presence known, as if to warn all mortals that they should never let down their guard.

Tragically, the house burned to the ground in an early morning fire in 1959. Perhaps only then could the spirit of Colonel William Preston at last rest in peace. But did it rest? In more recent years, amateur ghost hunters have investigated the grounds of Greenville. They reported recordings of unexplained sounds.

Fragments of Folklore

In the mid- to late 1930s and early 1940s, America was deeply mired in the Great Depression. In an effort to alleviate the situation, the federal government formed the Works Progress Administration, whose mission was to find jobs for the unemployed. One wing of the WPA hired writers to fan out across the country and record oral histories of people. Sometimes the narratives included paranormal subject matter, such as ghosts, witches, superstitions and supernatural happenings. One of the writers covering Roanoke and the surrounding area was a woman named Gertrude Blair. Following are a few of her stories, along with one from Lavelette Dillion.

A Cure for Witches' Spells

Blair interviewed Mrs. Eliza Seymour, her grandmother, who then lived in an "inaccessible fastness of the Back Creek section of Roanoke County":

> *I went up to help grandma pick her cotton and after supper I lighted the candles so as to see how to pick out the seeds. She came in from the kitchen, and, raising her hands in alarm, said, "Put out that light. Don't you know you can't have any light? As soon as it gets dark those pesky witches come snooping around! The logs burning there will give you plenty of light." So I had to sit on the floor in front of the fireplace and pick seeds from that cotton.*

The next morning she sent me to the barn to feed the horses. I noticed that "Betsy," the gray mare, just stood still and looked so droopy. Didn't touch a thing to eat, so when I went to the house and told grandma about it, whereupon she said, "I know those witches were here last night." She went out to see for herself, came back, and got some asafetida (the fetid gum of various oriental plants of the carrot family, formerly used in medicine as an antispasmodic, and in folk medicine as a general prophylactic against disease). She put some of this in a piece of white cloth, tied it up, and hung it on Betsy's neck.

Would you believe it, that horse was well in no time!

DON'T MESS WITH A MARKER STONE!

For this account, WPA writer Gertrude Blair climbed halfway up a mountain just outside Roanoke to interview a farmer named Joe Adkins. She apparently was impressed with the location:

The air was deliciously invigorating, perched as we were so precariously on the side of the mountain. Mr. Adkins cut the logs right off the land nearby and built his house. In traveling through these mountains and hollows, one notices every inch of level ground is cultivated. Snap beans, Irish potatoes, cabbage, beets, tomatoes, etc., are planted in little patches and grow to great perfection, owing to the rainfall on the steep mountain sides, carrying the moisture and rich loam with it as it washes to the level below.

Adkins was a noted storyteller in the area, and he told Blair the following, which he said was true:

A man on the mountain once moved a stone, marking the boundary line between his land and his neighbor's, giving himself some of his neighbor's land. Long after the man died, people could see him standing I the vicinity, holding the stone, saying, "where should I put it?" One day an old lady angrily cried out, "put it back where you took it from!"

As the shade of the man passed her, her apron touched the stone and it burned it! The stone was put back in its original place. You can't move a landmark, or there'll be a curse on your family. I know people right here in the mountains that have had a curse on them to the fourth generation for moving a landmark.

THE HAUNTED TAVERN

WPA writer Lavalette Dillon recorded this legend of a haunted tavern on Route 220 between Troutville and Fincastle, a scant few miles north of Roanoke, on May 22, 1936. The building dated to 1793:

> *There once was a large frame tavern run by a man named John Kesler. He was one of the early German settlers in the area and probably came in the 1780s or earlier. The tavern was on a road which was once the main highway to the southwest. Travelers, adventurers, and merchants often stopped here overnight, as the tavern was large, comfortable and conveniently located.*
>
> *Two men driving hogs south spent the night here and were never heard from again. It was rumored that they had been murdered for their money, and it was after their disappearance that the tavern was said to have become haunted. The wife of one of these men came to Virginia in search of her husband, and discovered a black horse grazing in Kesler's field, which she identified as having belonged to her husband. The tavern keeper contended that the animal was a stray horse he had found and knew nothing of its owner. The lady never had a chance to carry the matter further. Kesler shot and killed her! He was tried for murder and acquitted on the grounds that the shooting was accidental.*
>
> *After that, strange noises were heard in the middle of the night, and barrels of wine and whiskey were found smashed and overturned, their contents covering the cellar floor. No clue to the mystery could be found, but it was whispered that ghosts lurked among the shadows and cobwebs of the cellar, and evil rumors were insinuated about John Kesler.*
>
> *After Kesler died, the old tavern was turned into a private home, later deserted, and finally torn down about 1906. A young man digging in the cellar floor of the departed tavern, in search of suspected hidden gold, uncovered two skeletons bleached dry with age.*

Note: These accounts have been recounted here with the permission of the Blue Ridge Institute in Ferrum, Virginia, where many of the WPA records are kept.

THE LAST PUBLIC HANGING IN VIRGINIA

If ever a man had just cause to return in ghostly form to right a wrong rendered to him in life, that person might well have been John Hardy of Roanoke. Here is his true story.

In the dark, late-night hours of October 12, 1906, three Roanoke police officers, without warrants, stormed into the Alleghany Institute, a former boys' school that then housed African American tenants. It was a site that the local newspaper called "a harbor for thieves and criminals." The stated purpose of the officers' raid was that they were "looking for thieves." An old woman pointed them to a single apartment. When they pounded on the door and no one answered, they forced it open and, with guns drawn, walked into a scene of confusion.

The shocked Hardy scrambled to put on his trousers, while a woman lay in bed. The officers announced that they were under arrest, for apparently no specific reason, and Patrolman Robert Beard, who was white, was left to hold them, while the two others left the room to search elsewhere. As they did, one of them said, "If that n----- makes a crooked move, shoot him!"

It is at this point that versions of what happened next vary critically. Hardy claimed that when he went to get his coat, Beard opened fire on him, and he, in turn, returned the fire, hitting the officer three times, once in the chest, killing him. Later, at a subsequent trial, the prosecutor contended that Hardy had ambushed Beard. The only witness, the woman, said that she had hidden in the closet when the police burst in and didn't see who shot first.

Hardy then bolted out the door and ran down the hall. The other two officers saw him and fired away, wounding him in the thigh. He managed to limp out of the building and escaped in the countryside. Townspeople were enraged, and a manhunt that included search dogs was hastily organized.

Four days later, farmers on neighboring Bent Mountain saw Hardy, surrounded him and beat him mercilessly with shovels, pitchforks, clubs and pistols. He also was shot through the cheek and jaw and lost an eye. After Hardy was captured and jailed, he was asked why he had fled. He answered, "Because they are so bad about lynching folks around here." Indeed, he was right. Racial tensions ran high at that time, and there had been incidents where African American men in the area had been badly beaten or lynched. Only two years earlier, when a woman and her daughter had been brutally attacked by a black stranger, rumors and tempers ran wild, and one innocent man was tied to a telephone pole and lashed with electric wires. Eleven years before that, another man had been lynched in public and his body riddled with bullets and then burned during the infamous Roanoke riot of 1893. Such scenes of horror drew large crowds of curious spectators.

As a precautionary measure, Hardy was sent to jail in Wytheville. One month later, he appeared at his trial in Roanoke, with a patch over his lost eye and scars all over his head and body. Defense lawyers said that their client should be freed because the officers who conducted the raid had no warrants, and Hardy had a right to defend himself. The prosecutor said that there was no evidence that officer Beard had even fired a shot. The jury, however, took only forty minutes to find the defendant guilty of first-degree murder. Hardy was sentenced to death by hanging. Appeals were denied. The night before the hanging, Hardy told a newspaper reporter, "When I die, it will be for killing a man in self-defense."

Over the time between the trial and the execution, public sympathy seemed to shift in Hardy's favor. Petitions were signed to commute his sentence to life imprisonment, and the signatures included prominent citizens, as well as two of the jurors! Nevertheless, it was no surprise when Governor Claude Swanson failed to act in Hardy's behalf.

On the day of his hanging, it was reported that his fellow inmates wept as he was led to the gallows. Then, cruel fate intervened. As reported at the time, "As Hardy shot downward, the rope snapped on the beam and he fell in a heap. There were gasps of unbelieving horror from the spectators who had gathered in the Roanoke jail yard. The body rolled over without a groan or a twitch." Hardy was revived from his unconsciousness and led back up the scaffold. Then another twist developed. One of the attending police officers fell through the trapdoor as he adjusted the rope.

Finally, John Hardy was swung into eternity. There is no report of his ghost returning to haunt those who beat and abused him and hastened his untimely and possibly unjust death. Perhaps he rests in peace, somehow aware that his execution was the last public hanging to be held in Virginia.

The Little Rag Doll

The origins of the following legend trace back to a rural district in the greater Roanoke area of southwest Virginia early in the 1900s. It has been passed down ever since, from generation to generation. A new teacher for the local elementary school had been abruptly summoned when the previous teacher suddenly, unexpectedly and without a word of explanation quit on the spot and left the region, after appearing to be visibly shaken to the core.

Curiously, the principal told the new young woman that she had to leave the school each afternoon no later than 2:30 p.m. No reason was given. Odd, she thought, but she followed the instruction, and everything went smoothly for two months. As Thanksgiving was approaching, however, the teacher became absorbed in making plans for a holiday play and, not noticing the time, stayed past the deadline.

Precisely at 3:00 p.m., she heard the unusual call of a strange bird and then felt an unearthly chill. The room temperature dropped thirty degrees. The teacher looked up from her desk, and there stood an ashen-faced wraith of a little girl, about eight or nine years old. She seemed to have materialized out of nowhere. In a faint voice, the girl whispered, "Teacher, what is my homework and where is my rag doll?"

Startled, the woman stood up, and the girl, apparently frightened, ran out of the room, dropping a book on the floor as she did. Instantly, the room temperature returned to normal. The teacher picked up the book. Nearly worn out, it had been published in the 1890s and was long out of use. The teacher went to the principal and told her what had happened. The older woman seemed angered that her rule of not staying past 2:30 p.m. had been broken, but she said nothing else.

That night, the teacher decided to hand-stitch a rag doll in case the girl came back. The next day, she purposely stayed late, and the same eerie scene was repeated. She heard the bird call, the temperature in the room plummeted and the little girl entered the room. She again asked about her homework and her rag doll. The teacher told her to read the first three pages in her book and said, "Here is your doll," handing both items to the girl. Then the girl turned toward the door and vanished.

The teacher went back to the office, and this time the principal took her by the arm and said, "Let's take a walk." They went through a patch of woods, and the principal told the teacher that many years ago, a nine-year-old girl went to their school. One day, while playing in a creek after school, she slipped, hit her head on a rock, fell into the icy water and drowned.

The two women walked a little farther, to a small graveyard, where they saw a tombstone with a tiny angel on top of it. The inscription read, "Emily Caldwell: Born 1902—Died 1911."

BIBLIOGRAPHY

Anderson, Eunice. Personal interview, October 22, 2002.

Barnes, Raymond. *History of the City of Roanoke.* Roanoke, VA: Commonwealth Press, 1968.

Bell, Carroll. Personal interview, July 30, 2012.

Carvelli, Deborah. Personal interview, August 12, 2002.

Dean, Donna. Personal interview, August 14, 2002.

De Messiner, Sophie. *There Are No Dead.* Boston, MA: Sherman French & Company, 1912.

Firebaugh, Kathy. Personal interview, August 13, 2002.

Hall, Doug. Personal interview, August 12, 2002.

Hare, Joseph. *The Outlaw Years.* New York: Literary Guild of America, 1930.

Hunter, Frances. "Buried Sitting Up." "Frances Hunter's American Heroes" blog, May 10, 2010.

Library of Virginia. *The Life of Joseph Hare.* Pamphlet. Self-published, 1818.

Loveland, Louise. Personal interview, November 2, 2002.

Maxwell, Eddie. Personal interview, September 9, 2002.

Reiley, John. Personal interview, September 8, 2002.

Roanoke Times. "Hunting for Haunted," October 17, 2007.

———. "Recalling the 'Yarb Doctor.'" October 22, 2012. Roanoke.com.

———. "Roanoke's Last Public Execution." June 14, 2007. Roanoke.com.

———. "Still Perking." October 22, 2012. Roanoke.com.

———. Various articles. March 1902.

Shepard, Carol. Personal interview, November 10, 2002.

Taylor, L.B., Jr. *Ghosts of Virginia.* Vols. 1–13. Williamsburg, VA: self-published, 1993–2007.
Virginia Landmarks Register. University of Virginia Press, Charlottesville, Virginia, 1999.
Virginia Museum of Transportation, ghost tour, October 1998.
Vought, Mary. Personal interview, August 24, 2002.
Webb, Cathy. Letter to the author, September 13, 2002.
Works Progress Administration, various folklore papers, 1936–41. The Blue Ridge Institute, Ferrum, Virginia.

ABOUT THE AUTHOR

L.B. Taylor Jr. is a native Virginian. He was born in Lynchburg and has a BS degree in journalism from Florida State University. He wrote about America's space programs for sixteen years for the National Aeronautics and Space Administration (NASA) and aerospace contractors before moving to Williamsburg, Virginia, in 1974 to be public affairs director for the BASF Corporation. He retired in 1993. Taylor is the author of more than three hundred national magazine articles and fifty nonfiction books. His first book, *Pieces of Eight: Recovering the Riches of a Lost Spanish Treasure Fleet*, published in 1966, is still in print. Taylor's research for the book *Haunted Houses* (published by Simon & Schuster in 1983) stimulated his interest in area psychic phenomena and led to the publication of twenty-five books on Virginia ghosts. In 2007, he was presented the Lifetime Achievement Award by the Virginia Writers' Club.

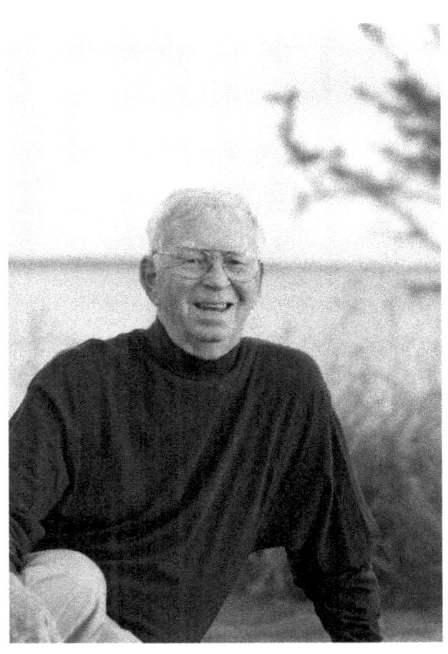

Photo by Michael J. Westfall.

www.ingramcontent.com/pod-product-compliance
Lightning Source LLC
LaVergne TN
LVHW052342100826
845147LV00021B/1150

9781609499433